JESUS

TEXT BY EUGEN WEILER

PHOTOGRAPHS BY ERICH LESSING

JESUS

A PICTORIAL HISTORY
OF THE NEW TESTAMENT

A CROSSROAD BOOK

THE SEABURY PRESS · NEW YORK

1980
The Seabury Press
815 Second Avenue
New York, N.Y. 10017

Jesus: A Pictorial History of the New Testament by Eugen Weiler and photographs by Erich Lessing, translated from the German by Matthew J. O'Connell from the original German *Jesus Gottessohn* © copyright 1974 Verlag Herder KG, Freiburg im Breisgau. English edition © copyright 1975, Franciscan Herald Press.

Library of Congress Catalog Card Number: 80-51760

ISBN: 0-8164-2287-7

Preface

This book is meant for the many who are seeking God. To seek God is to seek the supporting ground of human life and the goal of that life which is eternal fulfillment. As we go our way, God has already come to meet us, for he tells us, in Pascal's words: "You would not be looking for me if you had not already found me." In Jesus God has taken the extraordinary step of entering as a man into the field of our human experience. The aim of this book is to lead the reader to Jesus, so that we may find him and say to him with Simon Peter: "Lord, to whom shall we go? You have the words of eternal life. We have come to believe; we are convinced that you are God's holy one" (Jn 6:68), and so that through community with Jesus we may find what we are looking for: God.

Our aim is to awaken faith, hope, and love, so that we too may have the "great joy to be shared by all the people" (Lk 2:10). Since the book is also meant for meditation, we have thought it appropriate to add pictures to the text.

I gratefully dedicate my part in this book to my parents, my friends, and the many others who have shown me the way and travelled it before me or with me.

Eugen Weiler

"But when the designated time had come..." (Gal 4:4)

If we are to understand the activity of Jesus and the often large crowds of followers of whom the gospels tell us, we must first try to visualize the situation in Palestine at the time of Jesus' birth.

Since 63 B.C. Palestine had been part of the Roman Empire, and Roman garrisons were quartered throughout the country. The high priests and supreme council (Sanhedrin) at Jerusalem still functioned as the highest civil and religious authority. Many Jews, however, on both religious and national grounds, were scandalized by the country's dependence on Rome, the presence of pagans in the form of occupation forces, and the growing influence of Greco-Hellenistic (pagan) culture.

The Sadducees, who formed the propertied class and held almost all the higher offices, including that of the high priesthood, favored a policy of adaptation to the Roman presence. This was their reason for prosecuting Jesus as an insurgent, for they feared a punitive reaction by the occupation forces.

The Pharisees, the second most important class of Jews, resisted every attempt at assimilation. They were men who stood strictly by the Torah or law of Moses and kept their distance from all who were less rigidly observant, especially the "ignorant crowds." It was for this reason that they were called "pharisees," that is, "separated." Since they obeyed the law exactly not only in the privacy of their homes but in public as well, they were highly regarded by the people. Most of the scribes, or men knowledgeable in the Scriptures, were Pharisees, and through them the Pharisees as a class exercised a strong influence on the supreme council.

The preservation of pure doctrine was more important than political independence to the Pharisees. In their view the coming of the Messiah and consequently the redemption of Israel depended on unconditional, literal observance of the Mosaic law. In practice, this attitude led the Pharisees into forms of fidelity to law that we today find grotesque, as, for example, in their conflicts with Jesus over the Sabbath rest and tithing. In fact, we run the risk of overlooking the earnest efforts of the Pharisees to practice true love of God and neighbor and of forming our judgment of them solely in the light of the many bizarre positions they took. But that would be to do them an injustice.

Large groups of Jews in Jesus' time thought the end of the world was close at hand. They were convinced that the coming of the Messiah was imminent. He would restore Israel and David's kingdom and would make Yahweh's lordship evident to all mankind. The hopeless distress of broad strata of the population fostered expectations that Yahweh must at last intervene by sending his anointed one, and we find these ideas, hopes, and desires being disseminated in numerous non-Biblical writings of the time. They had an influence that can hardly be exaggerated, and affected the teaching even of the Pharisees and other religious groups.

Jesus and his message are unintelligible except against this background. After all, he was not born just "somewhere" and "at some time or other," but became a real man, "born of a woman, born under the law" (Gal 4:4), at this particular time and in this particular place.

Of the childhood of Jesus the gospels of Mark and John tell us nothing and the gospels of Matthew and Luke very little. What the latter do have to say is told for a definite purpose: to show that the promises are now fulfilled. "When the designated time had come, God sent forth his Son" (Gal 4:4).

The stories that take shape around the birth of Jesus capture and express the truth about him: He is from God and his real origin is in God. Essential themes in Jesus' future preaching are already introduced in a summary way in the infancy stories: This Jesus is sent to the poor, the sinners, the lost, the outcast. Even the pagans are invited to worship God and to bring their gifts, that is, themselves. This child, whose name means "God saves," is God's gift to mankind; he is the sign of God's gracious favor and his will to establish peace. Therefore, Christians throughout the centuries have believed that their Christ is man, like us in everything, and that he is also God's Son.

The infancy and childhood of Jesus were like those of every other Jewish boy. His parents had him circumcised; they presented him in the temple; and when he was twelve years old they took him with them to celebrate the Passover at Jerusalem.

Here, at this very important point in the life of a Jewish youth, Jesus showed his parents that he was travelling a very definite road and following a secret inner call: He will be—must be—about his Father's business. What God wants of him, he will do; he will live his life as God wants him to. What he does now and will do in time to come will not necessarily fit in with the ideas and expectations of men, not even those of his parents. That is the chief point this episode makes clear to us.

Christians did not begin until relatively late to celebrate the birthday of Jesus whom they acknowledged as their Lord. The reason is that they lived with their eyes on the exalted Lord and looked forward to his return. Easter, the resurrection, was and still is the real supreme festival of the Church and Christians. Nonetheless, we are fully justified in celebrating the birth of Jesus if we look at it with the eyes of faith and see in Him the sign of God's love become man for us. And it is meaningful to exchange gifts on this day when the exchange is an expression of our joy and our gratitude for God's love which we experience in Jesus and which is "to be shared by all the people" (Lk 2:10).

The pictures on the following pages are of:

"Proclaiming the Good news" (Mk 1:14)

John ("Yahweh has shown mercy"), son of the priest Zechariah, of the tribe of Levi, and his wife Elizabeth, had been at the Jordan preaching a baptism of repentance that would lead to the forgiveness of sins. He was conscious of having been called by Yahweh ("I am, who am"). Evidently, many took him for the Messiah or at least for his forerunner, Elijah returned to earth. But John thought of himself differently: "The testimony John gave . . . was the direct statement, 'I am not the Messiah'" (Jn 1:19-20). In his own eyes he was "a voice in the desert, crying out: Make straight the way of the Lord" (Jn 1:23). John had collected a large crowd of followers who made his proclamation their own and spread it abroad.

The activity of John the Baptist

John did not anticipate that the Messiah (the Christ or "anointed one") would come in poverty and lowliness. That is why, later on, he would have his disciples ask Jesus: "Are you 'He who is to come' or do we look for another?" (Mt 11:4). Jesus sent back the answer that he was indeed the one promised by the prophets.

According to the New Testament picture of him John stands squarely in the prophetic tradition. Repentance for him does not mean carrying out a list of demands nor is it an outward action such as a sacrifice. Repentance is a change of mentality, a conversion of the heart or innermost depth of a man's being. Only through such a conversion, John says, can a man escape the final condemnatory judgment that is imminent. At the same time, however, John is not satisfied with generalities but tells his hearers quite specifically that repentance means listening to Yahweh and giving every man his due (Lk 3: 10-14). The requirements John sets forth are, of course, conditioned by his own situation, yet they are also valid for our own day. Share your food with the hungry! Do not cheat your fellow man! Do not use your power or position to the disadvantage of others! Who can say that such principles are outdated?

John lived what he preached. That is why he had such an effect on people: his character was evident and attracted men strongly. He summoned everybody to face God as he was. He did not go easy on anyone. He made no effort at accommodation, did not water down his demands in order to gain a hearing, made no concessions even to the powerful or to special interest groups. It is easy to understand why those awaiting the Messiah were enthusiastic at his preaching and many were moved to conversion.

The baptism of Jesus

Among the many who came to John at the Jordan was Jesus of Nazareth; it is even likely that he spent some time with him. When Jesus had been baptized, his hour struck: "Suddenly the sky opened and he saw the Spirit of God descend like a dove and hover over him. With that, a voice from the heavens said, 'This is my beloved Son. My favor rests on him'" (Mt 3:16-17). According to Mark and Matthew only Jesus sees the dove descending from heaven; according to Luke all can perceive it.

We want to know—in fact, that is almost our sole interest—just what Jesus, or Jesus and the crowd, experienced. But that is unimportant to the evangelists. Their concern is to make it clear that the Spirit from above, the Holy Spirit himself, and not John or his baptism, has commissioned Jesus and empowered him for his mission. It is by the power of the Holy Spirit that Jesus is now to begin his work, preach to men, and show them by example what his own experience has been and what his mission is. In so doing he will act in accordance with the will of God the Father.

Jesus in the wilderness.

The Holy Spirit now led Jesus into the lonely wilderness. Perhaps he had been there before. We do not know how long he stayed there on this occasion, but does time play any really significant role in such events? Is not the very question of time irrelevant? To raise it is to stay on the surface of things and to miss what is really important.

One of Martin Buber's Hasidic tales "explains" exactly what Jesus was doing at this time:

> When Levi Isaac returned from his first journey to Rabbi Schmelke, which he had made against his father-in-law's wishes, the latter pressed him: "Well, what did you learn from him?" Levi Isaac answered: "I learned that the world has a Creator." At that the old man called one of the servants and asked him: "Did you know that the world has a Creator?" "Of course, I did!" the servant answered. But Levi Isaac cried: "O, everybody says that, *but do they know it from their own experience?*"

Jesus learned from experience to be obedient, that is, to live *entirely* for God and men. He learned from experience how to be God's voice and revelation.

Jesus here in the wilderness is like many great men before and after him; we need think only of the prophets, Paul, or many of the saints. He needs silence, solitude, "the wilderness." During these days he gains a clear vision of the mission the Father has entrusted to him: he must become entirely the one whom God and men need, entirely and exclusively the voice of the Father, for he himself is his mission.

We do not have to know what went on within Jesus during this time, what he had to struggle with and persevere through until he became God's messenger in all the purity and transparency that are his as the gospels portray him. All the evangelists do tell us, however, that this was a time of great temptation. What little they report concerning this time affords us deep insight and is quite enough for anyone who knows the importance of solitude and silence in his own life. In times of stillness urgent questions force themselves upon us; we cannot evade them, provided, of course, we are determined to think them through to the end.

One such question is the importance of material things in a man's life. Jesus faces this question in a very concrete form, for he has become extremely hungry. Does he not have the right to sustain his life?

Another question: Is he, as the Son, not master of the world? Shall he exercise his power and carry out his mission in the way people expect? Is not Psalm 2:8 an invitation to him: "Ask of me and I will give you the nations for an inheritance and the ends of the earth for your possession"?

Still another question: Should he not leap down from the pinnacle of the temple in order to show his trust in God and assure himself that God is indeed with him? Hasn't God urged him to do so? Wouldn't that make his identity clear to the whole people? Must God, will God, not manifest and accredit the Messiah in this fashion?

Jesus fights off the temptations. In the ebb and flow of temptation's onslaught upon him God's will becomes ever clearer to him. He learns what it means to be the Son of the heavenly Father, learns where the road of life is leading him. He becomes the man who seeks nothing for himself and looks to God for everything, the man who puts his life wholly in God's hands so that he may receive it from God's hands. He becomes the man who refuses to bring God's kingdom on earth by earthly means: weapons or power or "diplomacy," the man who needs neither miracle nor magic nor similar confirmation from God. He is God's Son! He believes in God's communion with him, God's "Yes" to him. And in so doing he honors the Father and prays to him "in spirit and truth" (Jn 4:24).

Anyone who knows how easy it is for a man to fool himself, and how quickly he can mistake his own will for God's and carry it out in God's name can probably appreciate what Jesus went through at this time in order to become what he is for us. We know that he will never waver in the decision he made; for him there is no turning back. He himself acted as he later required others to act: "Let the dead bury their dead; come away and proclaim the kingdom of God" (Lk 9:61).

Jesus' decision and his determination are important to the evangelists. His decision is to draw his life from God alone and to live it for God alone and therefore solely for his glory. In concrete terms this means that in every situation he will listen to God and obey him; it means obedience to the point of dying. It is this attitude of Jesus that will cause people later on to ask: "Who is this man?" He isn't like the scribes, for he proclaims God's word with authority! Evidently this was a new experience for these people. It is an experience which alert hearers of God's word have even today: that the man who speaks is as important as what is said and that word must match conviction.

Jesus' public life

After the time in the wilderness, Jesus went to Galilee—"in the power of the Spirit" (Lk 4:14)—and began to preach, probably in the synagogues to begin with. The general expectation of the Messiah's coming provided him with a starting-point.

"Jesus appeared in Galilee proclaiming the good news of God: 'This is the time of fulfillment. The reign of God is at hand! Reform your lives and believe in the gospel'" (Mk 1:14-15). The decisive moment, determined and brought to pass by God, is now here. This is God's hour! This is the day of fulfillment! (Cf. Lk 4:21.) God is acting through me, he is at work in what I do. With this claim Jesus forces his hearers to their own decision, for a Jew had to choose: "Anyone who talks this way is either making a monstrous claim or is truly sent by God."

Today, the word "lordship" or "kingship" can easily lead to rather gross misunderstandings. Prejudices and instinctive rejections that spring from our age and circumstances come into play when we hear such words.

Israel had its own idea of God's lordship, derived from its historical experience. That lordship was originally conceived in nationalist terms, but even then it always referred to a kingdom of justice and peace for all. In the case of Jesus and even of John the Baptist the nationalist elements have been eliminated. Nowhere does Jesus say that God's kingdom is coming in Israel or that he will establish such a kingdom. One aspect of Israel's expectations, however, Jesus does share: only God can bring about God's kingdom in which all men will be able to respond to their divine vocation in happiness and peace, free of anxiety and trouble and the powers of evil. For God alone is Lord!

Kingdom of God

The kingdom of God is both present and future. It is already here, yet in its full form it is still coming. It grows in the course of history to its perfection, and therefore in its full form it has not yet come.

Jesus breaks with all previous ideas and images of the kingdom by proclaiming that in his own activity God has already begun his rule. In Jesus who stands before them the rule of God is already here. In encountering Jesus men can experience and "see" what God's kingdom and rule mean. For in the coming of Jesus among them God invites all men to enter his kingdom by submitting to his rule. The kingdom, then, is not something in the distant future or in the next world, but is present now when men encounter Jesus and hear and accept his message. It is "already in your midst" (Lk 17:21). When men accept the message the kingdom of God is present. That is to say that when a man opens his heart and believes in God's unconditional love for him, when he realizes what this unqualified promise of God means for him, then God begins to rule and his saving will becomes efficacious. When a man believes in Jesus's message, he stops focusing his whole attention on himself and making himself the center of reality. He is no longer constrained to act in that way because he need no longer assert himself before God and his fellow man; he is no longer forced to save or justify himself, for he knows he has been accepted by God. This belief makes him free. Being free with the freedom of God's children he must now live as a child in God's presence and become a true man like Jesus. In the love of God and the security it gives, a man can grow and mature and bring forth fruit. That is why he should believe now and live and act now on the basis of his belief. No one should wait until he feels inclined or put off the decision until he has finished his other business. For: "Better for us to obey God than men" (Act 5:29). In the presence of Jesus much that earlier seemed unimportant becomes important, while much else becomes unimportant or secondary: perhaps family relationships, "serious obligations," plans, goals, and so forth.

Gospel—Good news

Through his life and actions Jesus calls men to faith in his message. If a man accepts the message, he experiences it's power within him, liberating him and bringing joy. Jesus summons men, then, to believe what he says about God (cf. Jn 8:32). In his own life the truth about this God becomes perceptible to men; in him God reveals that He is love. Therefore it is through Jesus that we believe in God. He awakens faith in us and becomes its guarantor. "Let us . . . persevere in running the race which lies ahead; let us keep our eyes fixed on Jesus, who inspires and perfects our faith" (Heb 12:1-2).

Encountering Jesus

Jesus calls on men to believe, but he often meets with unbelief. We see an example of this in Luke's detailed account of Jesus' first sermon in his native city (Lk 4:16-30).

On a sabbath day Jesus went to the synagogue, as was his custom. He exercised his right as an adult Israelite and read to the congregation from the prophet Isaiah. "The spirit of the Lord is upon me; therefore he has anointed me. He has sent me to bring glad tidings to the poor, to proclaim liberty to captives, recovery of sight to the blind and release to prisoners, to announce a year of favor from the Lord" (Is 61:1-2).

In using this text Jesus summarizes his own mission: He has the Spirit and is therefore the Messiah. He goes forth to meet the poor of every kind and to proclaim to them not judgment but a "year of salvation." In his preaching the Scripture will be fulfilled, for he brings salvation.

Those present ought to listen to him, believe him, and trust that he can do what he says he can. But they do not believe him. Don't they see before them only one of their own, the son of Joseph? They do not acknowledge that their "today" has come; they fail to recognize that their hour has struck, and they reject him and, with him, God's offer of salvation. In so doing they exclude themselves from salvation and pass judgment on themselves. Jesus then reminds them of Israel's past history in which the fathers of these men acted as they are now acting. For this, they try to kill him. Thus the people of Nazareth, with whom he had grown up, are the first to threaten him with death. The encounter ends in a split between him and his native city.

The Christian's life involves an encounter with Christ, and the manner of the encounter can be different for every individual. The one thing certain is that no matter how it happens it must lead to a decision, for Jesus always summons us to follow him. Every individual must give his own very personal answer; in fact he must be ever more bent on answering. Perhaps our journey through life is leading us only slowly and painfully and in a roundabout way to a genuine encounter with Jesus? In any event, if we do what he says, if we mull over his words and never think they have no more to say to us, then as the years pass we will begin to realize what he can be and wants to be for us in life and in death.

As we go, we will from time to time catch a glimpse of what it means to be "saved." Then Jesus becomes more than just a name for us; his very person becomes a confession that "God is salvation" and that "there is no other name . . . by which we are to be saved" (Acts 4:12). At the same time, how many ups and downs will we not have to experience and how much will we not have to strip ourselves of, if we are to be ready for this ever deeper encounter with Jesus, for this friendship with him! And how many "lands of slavery" will we not have to abandon, because he summons us to leave behind whatever hinders us on our journey with him to the Father! "Believe in the gospel" means, therefore, "Have faith in God and faith in me" (Jn 14:1).

Jesus says nothing about any general improvement of the world, or about a revolution. He requires that a man begin with himself, because God has already made a new beginning with him and intends to give him the Spirit. A man must learn to derive his life from this Spirit and thus from God. If he does this, he will become fully human; if he perseveres, he will transform the world and its conditions so that God's kingdom and rule may reach their full form. In this way a man becomes what God wants him to be: He lets God be God and thus, to his own salvation, becomes a man on whom God's favor rests (cf. Lk 2:14). Then God will be all in all and for all (1 Cor 15:28).

The pictures on the following pages are of:

15 *The human Jesus (Greek icon, Athens)*
16 *Galilean vista, with Mt. Tabor in the distance*
17 *Stone jars found in Jerusalem*
18 *Sunrise on the Sea of Gennesaret*
19 *Wall of the temple in Jerusalem*
20 *Driving of the money-changers from the temple (column of baldacchino, St. Mark's Venice)*
21 *Country between Jerusalem and Jericho*
22 *The "Samaritan woman at the well" (Greek icon, Athens)*
23 *Pillars in a Herodian forum in Samaria*
24 *The synagogue of Capernaum*
25 *Mosaic with picture of temple curtain (synagogue at Tiberias)*
26 *Ruins of the synagogue at Arbel, west of Sea of Gennesaret*
27 *Hand of Jesus extended in blessing (detail of a Greek icon, Athens)*
28 *Cure of a blind man (Greek miniature)*
29 *Cure of a leper (Greek miniature)*
30 *Cure of a paralytic (Greek miniature, Athens)*

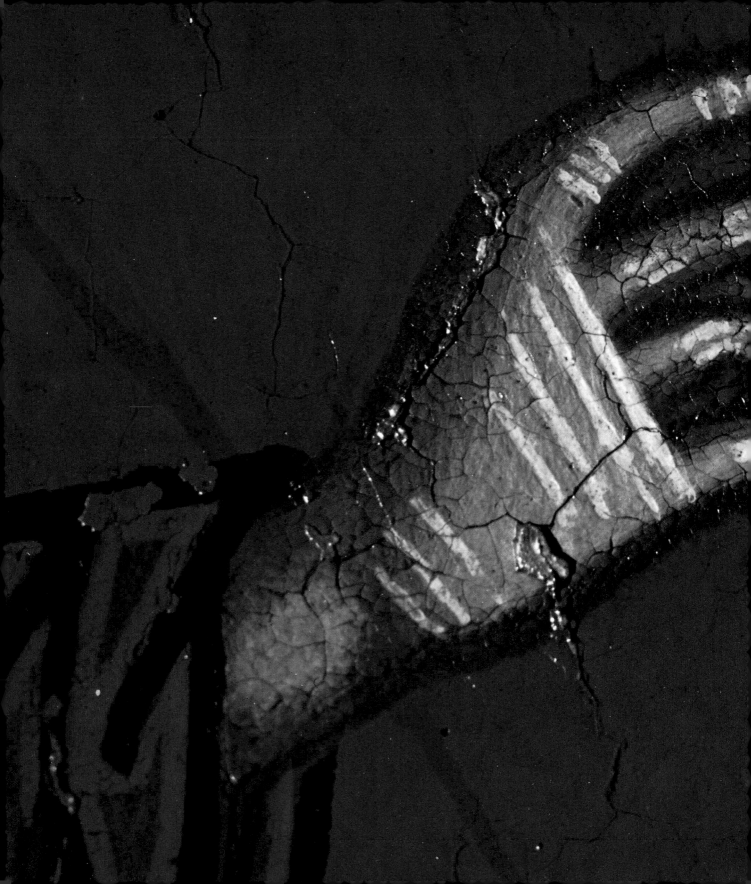

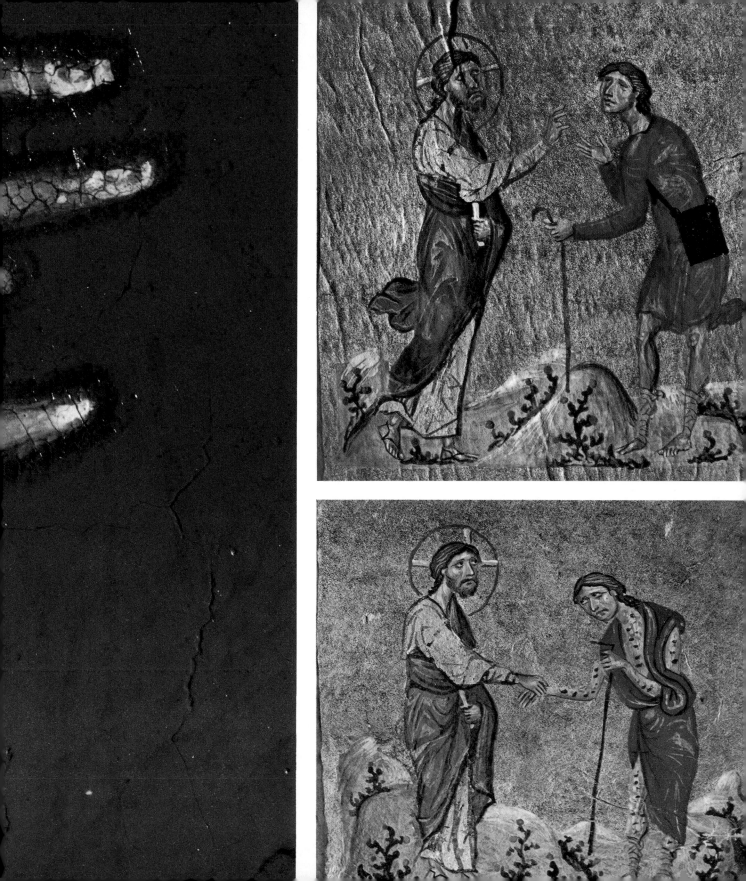

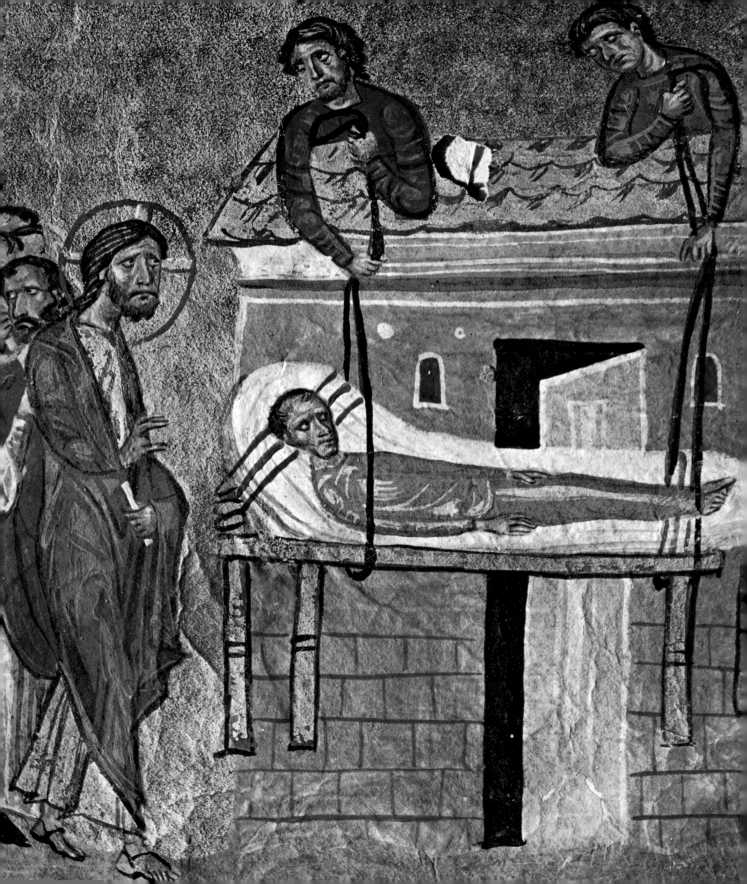

"And he began to teach them" (Mt 5:2)

The Sermon on the Mount is of central importance in the teaching of Jesus. Through the centuries indeed it has frequently been relegated to a secondary position, but on each occasion Christians came along who recognized once again its high significance and made it accessible to others.

What has happened in the history of the churches can also happen in the life of the individual believer. Many have passed by the treasure in the Sermon on the Mount without noticing it: perhaps because they had no one to act as a guide, perhaps because they hadn't looked for such a guide, perhaps even because they were unwilling to accept the requirements of Jesus' teaching.

The Sermon on the Mount

The Sermon on the Mount is not a carefully ordered body of teaching which the hearer or reader is forced to acknowledge as true. It is a sermon which the evangelist Matthew put together out of numerous sermons of Jesus. It is a proclamation, a call to faith, and an indication of the response this faith must give in everyday life. No one can fully grasp what Jesus is about and where he can lead his hearer, unless one enters into the Sermon not only with the understanding but also with the heart; in other words, to comprehend it fully one must put it into practice in one's daily life. Anyone who recognizes that Jesus is calling him, and is determined to follow, must realize that he is entering upon an adventure which will lead him he knows not where. We can see the truth of this statement from the lives of the saints; many of these lives will show us clearly how the Sermon can burst into a man's life, act upon it, and transform it.

The objections to the Sermon have always been the same: "All that doesn't apply today!" or "Where would we end up if we lived like that?" or "No one can ask all that of me!" They are about as weighty today as they have always been, even in the time of Jesus. Only if we stop taking ourselves so seriously, admit our helplessness, acknowledge our unwillingness, attach ourselves trustingly to Jesus, and remain with him, will we find the precious treasure (cf. Mt 13:45) that is hidden in the Sermon.

We must expend a great deal of effort and patience, we must listen, seek, and inquire into the meaning of Jesus' words in the various situations of our lives. In the Sermon, if anywhere in the Gospel, the issue is clear: Jesus' teaching will become intelligible and meaningful to us only if we *put it into practice*. It is one thing, for example, to speak of the love of one's enemies and to praise it as lofty virtue, and quite another to be sincerely kind to someone who is our enemy and hates us and runs us down. Jesus is asking for this kind of behavior as an authentic following of him.

The Beatitudes

The many individual sayings which make up the Beatitudes are related to various situations of everyday life, and are as varied as human life itself. The important thing for us is to grasp the spirit that speaks in them all.

Jesus (with divine authority!) calls blessed, or happy, those who must suffer the injustices and misfortunes of this world without being able to do anything about them. How many men have to endure spite and injustice from others! How many are persecuted for their convictions (or persecute others for theirs)! Think of all the things men do (and have done at every period of history) to each other out of habit and thoughtlessness, out of their need to feel important, out of vengefulness, anger, bitterness, or meanness! Jesus calls those happy who, no matter what men do to them or others, retain their trust in God and therefore do not return evil but rather act as the heavenly Father does: "This will prove that you are sons of your heavenly Father, for his sun rises on the bad and the good, he rains on the just and the unjust" (Mt 5:45).

Jesus says "Happy they" who, when faced with the evil and wretchedness of the world, live with God's loving kindness as their model and convey it to others, and who effect peace and reconciliation between men and are merciful. In their persons God takes the part of the humiliated and oppressed. On the last day, in the final judgment, God will justify men's trust in him, for their trustful Yes to God, in often impossible situations, is an act of faith in his fidelity. It is an act of faith in God as God: the one who can do all things and who will dry every tear.

Happy the poor

One of the Beatitudes deserves special attention.

"How blest are the poor in spirit: the reign of God is theirs (Mt 5:3). We might also translate: "Happy are . . ." or "Salvation is for. . . ."

According to Matthew, Jesus extols those who are poor within themselves, poor in God's sight, those who know that without God they are nothing and depend entirely on his mercy, so that they accept everything and their lives in their totality as his gift. This kind of poverty reflects the riches of God and his "emptying of himself" to men. (Here we have the very opposite of a degrading, unhealthy self-humiliation.)

According to Luke Jesus says simply: "Blest are you poor; the reign of God is yours" (Lk 6:20). Jesus requires that in such circumstances as we described above men should not turn away from God but rather expect everything from him. If a person lives by this kind of trust, he does not become passive or inactive; quite the contrary. God is with him! And this encourages a man to do everything he can in his situation. This kind of trust stimulates him to make every effort to master the situation, for it prevents surrender and resignation and enables him to see the genuine possibilities open to him. At the same time, however, it becomes clear that it is far more difficult to effect real change and improvement than first appeared. This is true of both individuals and peoples. This being the case, support and help can come only from a trust that God will keep his promises and that perseverance in time of difficulty has a genuine value which is often hidden from us at the moment but will become clear on the day of judgment.

The beatitude concerning the poor should not be isolated from the rest of Jesus' teaching. It is to be connected, for example, with what Jesus says elsewhere to his disciples: "As often as you did it for one of my least brothers, you did it for me" (Mt 25:40). Here Jesus takes his stand with the poor and identifies himself with those in need of help, so that he may remind his disciples of their obligations. Can there be a more radical way of moving men to help each other? Can there be a more urgent appeal to change harmful and evil situations, to eradicate their causes, and to have compassion on the world in its distress?

No Church and no individual Christian can ignore this beatitude without betraying Jesus. Isn't this especially true today when the test of concern is being applied to the disciple of Jesus? Today, when a tragedy or famine anywhere in the world becomes known to us so quickly and forcibly, excuses are hard to accept. Only action and honest effort have value. We Christians ought to be thankful that we are thus challenged and reminded of our duty! It clearly implies that men take seriously our message to the world.

The rich

Just as Jesus does not extol poverty simply as poverty (poverty as such is no virtue!), neither does he condemn wealth as such. Rather he insists in a very forceful way (in a way no one can evade, we might think) on the dangers which accompany riches. No one can close his eyes to the truth of the warning, or the "Woe to you rich" (Lk 6:24) will

be fulfilled. How easily, almost unnoticeably, a man loses his heart to the things he has, to his possessions! How readily the anxiety to cling to it all or even to augment it can preoccupy him and take him prisoner, so that he is deaf to God's call and to the distress of his fellowmen! Everyday we experience in ourselves and see in others how little difference it makes that we know: "Naked I came forth from my mother's womb, and naked I shall go back again" (Job 1:21). We know, too, that as we grow richer and more successful, our needs increase and, with them, the things that hinder us on the way to God; in other words, we have more to rid ourselves of, if we are to extend our freedom. At the same time, however, there are plenty of examples of wealthy Christians acting as "stewards" of their wealth for the benefit of their fellow-men; such Christians have not lost their souls because of their riches.

Right and wrong concern

The attitude that blocks entrance to the kingdom of heaven is that of continuous, absorbing concern for life, health, reputation, success, ability to compete, money in the bank, security. When this anxiety prevails, a man becomes a prisoner of himself and life passes him by. He loses his "I" or soul. The wrong kind of concern, which causes the loss of the soul or authentic life, can also be caused by anxiety lest we miss something in life and turn out a loser. In this case a man may in fact be fostering highly exaggerated expectations of life and his fellow-men; we often hear these in the form of: "I have a right to it, it's my due."

Jesus wants to help men rid themselves of such delusions so that they can find their firm footing and security in God, the Lord of life. If a man's life is thus "taken up" into God, thus hidden in God, he can with confidence live the length of life God has granted him. His whole attitude changes. He no longer asks: "What has life to offer me?" but "What does life, and God, expect of me?"

"Is not life more than food?" Jesus asks (Mt 6:25). What is life, after all? Jesus does not theorize about it but simply bids us live! But he does state a presupposition for living: to live by the gracious gift of God! He means that we must be convinced to the depths of our being that we owe our existence to God and that our life is a gift, a sharing in his life, love, and fulness of being. It is in that spirit that a man should live his life: now, at this moment, in the place where he now is. We can learn something of this attitude that Jesus is inculcating and try to put it into practice. We can ask ourselves, for example, whether we really need all the things we want or would like to have; whether many of them make us more dependent instead of more free, more open, more deeply responsive. We can also learn to do properly whatever we do; when we play we should play; when we work or eat or sleep, we should do these things and not be doing or wanting to do something different. In the various circumstances of life we can say: "Don't take yourself too seriously"; we can learn to laugh at ourselves, to see the humorous side of things and help others to see it.

The child as model

Jesus presents the child to us as a model of the right attitude toward life. Surprising, isn't it? The disciples wanted to keep children away from him, and here he is, making the child and its natural qualities an example for the disciples (Mt 18:2-4). He does not mean, of course, that we should remain children all our lives, nor is he thinking of the supposed innocence of children. His point is rather that just as children live their lives and accept the loving care of their parents, on whom they depend, as something self-evident and the basis for their lives, so the disciples should receive his life as a gift from God and live it as something fresh and new each day.

Something of this spirit shines through a story told about Don Bosco. He was playing soccer with his boys, when someone asked him what he would do if he knew he would die in half an hour; his answer, "Keep on playing"!

The genuineness of this attitude, which is that of authentic discipleship, is especially tested in difficulties and conflicts between men. The disciple will forgive someone who injures him, and not continue to bear a grudge; he will renounce revenge and violence. And the disciple will not focus his attention on what he may himself gain from such conduct or consider whether it is profitable to act thus; he will do what is good for the sake of the good!

Consistent to the end, Jesus asks us to love not only our opponent but even our enemy. "Show your enemies genuine kindness and love," he says. The love Jesus urges upon us is not a new kind of force or a refined way of ultimately subjecting other men to us; neither is it to be confused with the outlook of many who want the best for their fellow-men, no matter what it costs, and thereby only get on their nerves. It is not self-seeking, but is of the same nature as God's love, which it takes as its model.

Judge not!

In saying "If you want to avoid judgment, stop passing judgment" and "The measure with which you measure will be used to measure you" (Mt 7:1-2) Jesus has in mind an attitude that is so much part of us that we rarely notice it or, if we do, we notice it in others.

He is talking about our pre-judgments and judgments of others. Frequently we have already passed judgment on those with whom we must deal, and we stick to those judgments no matter what happens. How often we see in everyone and everything only or chiefly what is negative or bad, and then tell others about it! How often we tear others down in our own thoughts or in conversation and compare them with ourselves to their disadvantage! Isn't that frequently simply a form of prejudice? Why do we feel so insecure? Why do we feel ourselves so often challenged? Have we no alternative but to keep on shifting the responsibility to others?

Because Jesus was so sure of himself in and through God, he allowed other men to be what they were. He had no use for groundless generalizations about people, and for this very reason he became a true neighbor to all. This was the really surprising thing about him to many of his fellows: they were sure he really meant them well! As a result, he helped many to change their lives and begin anew. Through his faith in them he drew the good in them out of all its hiding-places; he trusted others in advance and thus made it possible for them to have trust: a profiteer, a prostitute, sick people, and healthy people too. He was genuinely kind.

By his own example Jesus has shown us the way. Anyone who wants to be his disciple must make a beginning and try to be to others what he would have them be to him. If we practice seeing and giving expression to the good in other people, this will have an effect on our own lives. We will become more joyous, learn to laugh at many human failings, and react more patiently to many things. What a help such a positive attitude to people would be in marriage, family, life, and friendships!

"Treat others the way you would have them treat you: this sums up the law and the prophets" (Mt 7:12).

In the Sermon on the Mount, then, Jesus is not interested in niggling rules for the everyday behavior of his disciples. He shows rather that his demands upon his disciples are so broad and comprehensive as to leave no area of human life untouched. His concern is with the spirit in which the disciple lives and acts. Yet it would be a false interpretation and miss the true meaning of Jesus' life and message to conclude that the disciple "must put up with everything, no matter what befalls him." Such an attitude would simply promote evil and make the disciple share the guilt of it. Many people would see in the Sermon only an exhortation to continue as they are.

Repayment

Always and everywhere Jesus opposed evil in an uncompromising way. He called evil evil and good good, and was concerned with the true manner of resisting evil. The disciple must learn not to repay evil with evil, hate with hate, a lie with a lie. He must learn to accept even "evil" men as his fellow men and to treat them with a genuinely pure intention. As a neighbor to others he must be always trying to determine which means are suited or unsuited for helping this enemy, this slander, or this "inconsiderate type" to effect a change of mentality in himself and acquire a new outlook. The future path and destiny of such men cannot be a matter of indifference to him. Such an attitude on his part is, admittedly, not possible unless he believes in the message of salvation and follows after Jesus. For, all too often, even the disciple is tempted to repay like with like: "You did it to me, I'll do it to you" (cf. Mt 5:38). Only faith will enable him in many a difficult situation to reject such a course and to prefer suffering injustice to causing it. Thus the disciple of Jesus will have to make his highest demands not on others but on himself.

Only from experience with himself and how he follows Jesus in one situation but fails to do so in another will the disciple learn to be patient, forgiving, kind, and understanding to others and thus continually break through the demonic vicious circle which evil creates. But everytime this happens, God's rule becomes a reality among men; the kingdom of God is present in our midst.

Reconciliation and peacemaking

Jesus calls peacemakers sons of God (Mt 5:9); later he says that those who love their enemies and pray for their persecutors are sons of God (5:44-45).

Now such statements violate what men call common sense; they are "against all experience and reason." But anyone who really hears and accepts the message of Jesus does not take such common sense for his guide but applies God's measure which Jesus, the Son of God, has shown us and lived out as an example to us. That measure is God's unconditional goodness that intends the good of all men, be they just or unjust. Consequently the disciple of Jesus is, in the eyes of many, an "incurable optimist" who lets nothing discourage him. He knows that he is himself entirely sustained by God's goodness and feels urged to share it with others. Therefore he tries to be a neighbor even to his enemy and by his attitude to move him to reconciliation and a shared "new beginning." His outlook may enable him to effect peace and reconciliation between third parties who are enemies to each other—people "who are no concern of his"!

The smallest act of reconciliation brings with it God's great promise: "They shall be called sons of God." For genuine community, mutual trust, and the heartfelt inclination to be kind to others, are infinitely precious to God, who is a God that loves men. And are not all men, openly or secretly, waiting for such kindness and love? The disciple is prepared to go out to others, to take the first step. In so doing, he becomes a light shining amid the darkness and sinfulness of the world (Mt 5:14). Because he thinks and speaks and acts in this way, he shares in Jesus and his mission and turns the thoughts of men beyond himself to God, the Father of light. "The man who continues in the light is the one who loves his brother" (1 Jn 2:10).

Jesus points in the same direction when he says: "If he holds him [his brother] in contempt he risks the fires of Gehenna" (Mt 5:22). Is there anyone who hasn't been shocked by these words? Jesus is not concerned simply with laws to protect the life of our fellowman; he is setting a new goal for us: brotherhood. Men are to live with each other and for each other, and thus make life more worthwhile, happier, richer, and easier for each other. Anyone who lives contrary to the interests of his fellow-man through malicious talk, anger, hatred, envy, and enmity makes life difficult or even insupportable for others and for himself; he scorns God's will and brings judgment upon himself.

There is no more important and urgent task than to rid the world of dissension and to bring about reconciliation where men have become divided. Not even the worship of God is a reason for deferring such reconciliation. In fact, less than anything else may divine worship be such an excuse, for it would draw down punishment on the one praying because of the living lie he represents and it would turn into an accusation against him.

We must note that the question of guilt in a quarrel or dispute is never raised. To raise it would hardly help toward reconciliation. The follower of Jesus is bound to do everything in his power to remove dissensions between men. Only if he makes an honest effort to do so does he take God seriously and honor him as Lord. "None of those who cry out, 'Lord, Lord,' will enter the kingdom of God but only the one who does the will of my Father in heaven" (Mt 7:21).

To act in this way undoubtedly takes self-conquest, fortitude, the courage of one's convictions, belief in goodness, and much else; in brief, it takes all the qualities faith makes possible for us. Only then is our worship worthy of God and our Christianity credible. What would happen if we Christians really took Jesus seriously?

Prayer

An important part of the Sermon in Matthew's gospel is what Jesus had to say about prayer. To this instruction belongs the Our Father which Jesus taught us as an example of the proper way to pray; it is also found in Luke, but in a shorter form (11:2-4). In Matthew's expanded version the Our Father clearly echoes the daily prayers said by Jews. The disciple is to pray for the coming of God's kingdom, which has now drawn near and indeed, in the preaching of Jesus "is at hand."

If we learn to pray as Jesus taught, it will affect all our prayer and petition. The important thing is not to use a great many words or to say a set number of prayers. What Jesus is teaching is the proper attitude to God the Father. Prayer is not to be understood as a business transaction: I give you something, and in return you give me a proportionate amount or, if possible, more. We are not to treat God as a means to the fulfillment of our desires.

The disciple prays for what he needs in order to sustain his life throughout this day, not for what would guarantee his needs being met in the more or less distant future. He asks for the forgiveness of his sins and is ready to forgive anyone who has wronged him, without calculating the extent of the wrong or keeping an account of it. He must not flee from the world but rather pray that while in it he may be preserved from the fearful temptation to stop believing in God and to become unfaithful; he must pray to be rescued from the evil one.

If a man prays for the coming of God's rule as Jesus teaches him to do, he is already submitting himself to that rule and is prepared to acknowledge in a practical way God's claim upon this world of his. He knows that dangers surround him but he also knows that God's power will sustain him.

Besides Jesus numerous personages in the Bible show us what an immediately understood thing prayer is for the believer and what it means to pray.

Prayer always involves both God and man, in an all-absorbing and often very passionate way. All pretence, exaggeration (the treacherous superlative!), and understatement are evidently false and unworthy. We must go as we are, with our good qualities and all our wretchedness, and speak with God, with the God and Father of Jesus Christ, that is, with the God of Abraham, and the God of Isaac, and the God of Jacob, the God of the fathers, not some higher being who has long since been domesticated by human thought. To pray, as the Bible understands prayer, is to make fully real the vital I-Thou relationship between man and God. It is to struggle and dispute and remonstrate with God, and refuse to let him go (Gen 32:27); it is to ask as a little child asks his mother; it is to be silent and listen, to be amazed and overwhelmed, to give thanks, to be joyous in God's presence.

"What do I do when I pray? I expose my soul to the sun."

Parable

Jesus wanted to present the message of the kingdom of God to his hearers—be they disciples, "the people," Pharisees, or scribes—in such a way that they could understand it. To this end he often made use of parables. The early Christian community repeated these parables or stories, but often to audiences that were very different from those Jesus addressed. As a result many parables acquired a new look and a different emphasis, and, consequently, additions were made to the texts themselves. For example, what in Jesus' mouth was a summons to faith and conversion on the part of the Pharisees acquired later on a new "vital context" (*Sitz im Leben*) when it was preached to the members of the Christian community. The same parable will acquire still a further new meaning when we apply it to our life today; and by "our life" I mean chiefly our life as a community. Jesus bases his parables on the everyday life of men, on their experiences, their joys and their sufferings. Everyone knows what it is for weeds to grow in with the grain, and would like to get rid of the weeds so that the grain might be stronger. Who has never heard of thieves or treacherous attacks and been afraid of them? Is there anyone who cannot understand the servant who had a huge debt canceled by his master and was very glad of it, yet could not bring himself to cancel a small sum owed him by one of his fellow-servants? Who has never been amazed at how over ambitious and cunning many people are? Who has not been annoyed by someone knocking late at his door, just when he was ready to go to sleep? These everyday experiences are important if people—including us today—are to understand the parables. Against the background of such experiences every hearer can say, as he hears the story, "Yes, that's how it is!" and can let himself be taken a step further. For it's not enough simply to know a parable. The intention of a parable is to affect us personally and make demands of us. We must go all the way with the parable, until we realize that amid the familiar realities of life the hidden reality of God's kingdom is breaking through into the light.

The parables conceal a mystery: the coming of God's kingdom into a world that gives little evidence of its presence. But if we are moved by the parable and realize that it speaks to our real situation, if we give a personal answer based on faith or say a wondering "Yes!" to it, then the kingdom of God is present among us.

Parable of the mustard seed

The parables of the mustard seed and the leaven (Mt 13:31-34) speak of this hidden presence of God's kingdom. The mustard seed is sown in the earth, grows, and becomes a tree in which the birds of heaven build their nests. A woman mixes only a little yeast with three measures of flour, but the little is enough to leaven the whole mass. Something is happening in both cases. The tiny thing turns into something very great; the invisible conceals the immense. It is an amazing action and we cannot comprehend it.

The disciple of Jesus must live by the conviction that God is at work. God's thoughts are not man's thoughts nor his ways man's ways (Is 55:8). The parable of the seed that grows of itself is intended to prevent us from thinking that by our own actions we can bring the kingdom of God to its completion. Just as the earth "by itself" produces a crop, so God's kingdom comes "by itself." Man cannot force it; he can only wait patiently for the harvest.

To wait in patience does not mean, of course, to fold one's hands and do nothing. The disciple must do what God's Spirit bids him do and thus cooperate by contributing his part. Jesus can therefore say: "Let him who has ears to hear me, hear" (Mk 4:9). The hearer must understand that he himself is, for example, the ground on which the seed of God's word falls so that it may develop its latent energies within him. He is not to be so concerned about the later fate of the seed as to forget that at the present moment he must receive it within him and allow it to grow. Here and now the summons reaches him; here and now he must obey it. That is his contribution to the kingdom of God!

The important thing is that we grasp the present, the now, of our life, and the significance of the present hour. Anyone who has even a little knowledge of the human heart knows how we human beings like to escape from the present moment, the present situation, the narrow limits of our life, into the world of possibilities: "If things were thus or so, then . . ."; "if I had. . . , I could do as I wished." He knows how often we shirk the burdens of the hour and the day, the things that should be done or said now and not put off. Everyone has experienced the temptation simply to let things slide ("what's the use of it anyway?") and to give up.

The message of Jesus forces us to look at the present moment: Every instant of life is an opportunity for man, but a risk as well. A man must use the opportunity! He must act as Jesus did! If he does, he will shape in an important way the next period of his life.

Once again, everyone has had experience which enable him to grasp what Jesus is saying: What great encouragement a good word at the right moment can bring; how devastating slander can be; how a word can have all sorts of good or evil effects.

"The world provides not only the place but even the object of man's authentic relationship with God. God speaks to him in the things and beings he sends into his life. Man responds by what he does with these things and realities" (Martin Buber).

Over and over again in the course of history the message of Jesus is brilliantly illumined by those of his disciples whom we call saints (whether or not they are officially recognized as such by the Church). Thus when Francis de Sales says that every moment of each God-given day is a task, he is expressing exactly what Jesus meant. He is talking of what would later be called the "little way" of Thérèse of Lisieux: the believer living in openness and readiness for every hint of God's will in his everyday life. The focus here is not on great deeds (unique and astounding accomplishments are relatively rare!), or on sacrifices that can impress even God, or on the mortifying of impulses that can easily spring to life again in another form. The important thing is fidelity to daily duties, small or great, accompanied by trust in God's help. "Great deeds will not always be ours to do. But each hour offers opportunities to do little things well, even very well, that is, with great love: to put up with the moods of others, to be meek and patient with people who are tactless, to master our own moods and inclinations, to overcome our depressions and antipathies. All that is far more salutary than we may think" (Francis de Sales).

No one is secure. A man may have failed a thousand times, then suddenly pull himself together and say, "Yes." Another may have long been faithful, then fall.

The prodigal son

Let us turn now to the parable of the prodigal son (Lk 15:11-32). It shows the father as a man of incomprehensibly great love. He ignores all the conventional restraints; reproaches have no place in his joy at his son's return. He makes his joy and unlimited love evident to the son, and the son is overwhelmed by it.

This younger son had left home and run through his inheritance in a foreign land. To survive, he had to hire himself out as a swineherd. Here he recognized his hopeless situation and unalleviated wretchedness, and "came to his senses." He said to himself: "I will break away and return to my father!" and he set out for home. He hoped that his father might take him on as a hired hand. Then his father came out to meet him and kissed him before he could say a word. The father accepted him back as his son! The son confessed his guilt and said he was no longer worthy to be a son; he confided in his father. He accepted his father's love and found himself home once more as a son, not as a hired hand. He celebrated the feast with the others and learned from experience what kind of man his father was.

The elder son did not understand what his father was doing, and did not join in the celebration. He did not see that his father's love was a vital necessity for his younger brother; the feast was in his eyes simply an act of unjustice and he began to make comparisons: "You never gave me so much as a kid goat to celebrate with my friends. Then, when this son of yours returns. . . ." He had lived for so long at his father's side, yet never learned what a father's love means. He had served and never disobeyed an order; but he had lived like a slave. But why had he not lived like a son, inspired by his father's love for him and his own filial love? Why had he never trusted his father and himself?

The father attempted to change his elder son's attitude and move him to share his own joy that his younger son, "this brother of yours," had returned home. He reminded him that "everything I have is yours." Everything belonged to him, not just the farm animals, but he had taken nothing for himself; he had understood nothing of the father's magnanimity and generosity, never made a claim on it. If he had, he would have seen what a man the father really was. He had never experienced the freedom of a son. But did this not mean that he had completely mistaken his father and missed the whole point of their relationship?

Did the elder son have any understanding of love and how it acts? He had never celebrated a feast, as he could and should have done. He had lived his life joylessly, even though he was in his own home! The younger son, on the contrary, had come to understand love. But the elder clung stubbornly to his views. Did he not thereby inevitably exclude himself from the happy companionship of the feast? Was not he, who had never left home, really the lost son? For he did not really "know" what it meant to be at home, and in the critical hour he excluded himself from it.

We who read this parable are asked where we stand and which of the two attitudes is ours. What of our love for the Father? Are we sons who accept the "everything I have is yours" and live in the full light of God's love? Or are we sons who have to be told: "You should have joined in the celebration and shared our joy!"?

The laborers in the vineyard

The parable of the laborers in the vineyard (Mt 20:1-16) is intended to teach us the same lesson: God's goodness is beyond all measure! If a man tries to calculate it or keep an account of it, he hasn't understood it at all, for he is measuring it by his own trivial human standard. What such a person is really thinking of is not love but performance. As long as he thinks that way, he will be scandalized, because the person who has out-performed others but is not better rewarded cannot but be scandalized. Therefore he thinks the estate owner acted unjustly.

What is the underlying problem? The workers who complain find their work a burden and an effort; they do not like doing it. In fact they say as much: we "have worked a full day in the scorching heat" and now we deserve higher pay. Aren't we modern Christians really like these workers, even if we don't intend to be? Don't we complain and protest in the same way? We make an honest effort to live as Christians, we deny ourselves a great deal, in short we bear the burden and heat of the day. What will our reward for that be? What more will we receive than the people who. . . .

The parable gives the answer to such questions: "I am free to do as I please with my money, am I not?" The answer is really not an answer but raises questions for us. Questions such as these: Hasn't the message of salvation brought you joy and enriched your life? Isn't the God who manifested himself in his Son a Father in whose house and under whose protection you have come alive and now enjoy prosperity? Are you not happy that you are with God and that he loves you?

Perhaps we are still far from having such an experience; perhaps we carry a lot of dead weight from childhood or schooling that renders access to God difficult; perhaps we are afraid to live by the "everything I have is yours." Perhaps we are afraid to live like Jesus! How many Christians there are who feel limited by their faith and think of it as a burden more than anything else. They see themselves only as surrounded by commands and prohibitions. Admittedly, it is not easy for people to break out of such a ghetto. And many, who do, do not find the freedom they seek but only build new walls around themselves, walls now to keep out God or Jesus or the Church.

Jesus' chief concern is that we should find joy. He describes that joy with many images: to be with the Father, to be allowed to work in the Father's vineyard. He has this joy in mind when he says that God is with us, wholly attentive to us and wholly favorable to us; that God wants to give himself to us and be everything to us that a man could desire; that his attitude to us is entirely uncalculating; that he rejoices over every person who finds him, and even wants to spend eternity with that person. All that can certainly make a man happy, and it will make him happy if he believes and accepts Jesus' word! It can sustain the believing disciple through all the vicissitudes of life and will be his hope when he is dying.

Jesus says: This God, the heavenly Father, requires no prior conditions of us and really lays no obligations on us. He is simply, infinitely, unfathomably good. He asks nothing of man but only wants to be something for man: his happiness and salvation! Therefore he makes man free and renders him capable of loving in return, voluntarily and whole-heartedly. Man is to love God as one loves who is free of all compulsions and burdens. That is what St. Augustine has in mind when he says: "Love, and then do whatever you want!"

The parable of the prodigal son challenges the disciple to become mature and free, a grownup son who lives as a true son in his father's house. To do this he must first have understood what love, free, self-giving love is. Shouldn't the man who has experienced what love is be happy and make this happiness the well-spring of his life?

A man's daily life will show whether he only knows how to talk about such love or, on the contrary, is really influenced by the miraculous experience of love. It is in daily life that the true disciple is manifested, that is, in love for the people with whom he lives and who come into contact with him. Thus the love between men and the good we do for one another are both a sign of the good news and a help to its better understanding.

We live by love

We know today how important the experience of human love and affection is for a child and his later life. We know too how much easier it is for a person to believe in the fatherly love of God if he has had the experience of being unconditionally accepted by another human being and has grown up in an atmosphere of genuine love. If men accept us and bestow their love on us, a way to God opens up before us; the radiance of God's infinite love shines through and he tells us he accepts us.

Yet how many children there are whom no one has accepted! What of them? It is true enough, of course, that our relationship to God does not terminate in our fellow man but goes through him to God. God is not reducible to our fellow-man, he is not simply identical with our neighbor. On the other hand we can encounter him in this world through our neighbor. For this reason a tremendous duty is incumbent on the disciple. He is bound to communicate to others the love he has received from God. Jesus calls this "serving." "Our duty as Christians consists in serving every man so that he may retain his true human dignity down to the last moment of his life" (Mother Teresa).

That is our responsibility today! Here too we have, beyond any doubt, the great task of the Christian community. It is a task which we, as a community, have hardly grasped as yet. After all, it makes little sense to talk of God's love to people and children who are knocked from pillar to post and whose only experience has been that no one wants them. It would be simply cynical for a prosperous man to confront a hungry one and tell him: "God wants you to be saved," while not giving him what he needs. Surely, too, we don't accomplish very much through charitable works, when frequently it is the conditions of society that must be changed if men are to be able to live lives worthy of human beings. This holds for the West no less than for the Third World. It is precisely in this area that the Church must prove her credibility and that of her message.

The sabbath

This is the proper context for bringing up the question of the sabbath. "Is it lawful to work a cure on the sabbath" (Mt 12:10; cf. also 12:1-8), Jesus asks the Pharisees. Their answer is an unqualified, "No." There were only a few, carefully regulated exceptions to the law of sabbath rest. According to God's will the sabbath was to be sanctified as a day of joy. But the day that was originally intended as a gift to man and beast; a protection against man's wilfulness, disregard, and exploitation had become in the course of time the exact contrary: a day of coercion and constraint, accompanied by the fear of violating the law and being punished.

Jesus' attitude shows him to be free of this constraint and sheds light on the original intention of the creator; God wants the well-being and salvation of men. The sabbath exists for man's sake, not man for the sabbath's. Jesus here requires his disciples to tear down the walls which time and circumstances or customs have erected and which now hinder man from being man, that is, creature and son of God. The disciple is to do away with everything that hinders man from being able to experience the Father's love. This means that the disciple must ask what the Father really wants. The Father has given the answer in Jesus, his Word made man.

The pictures on the following pages are of:

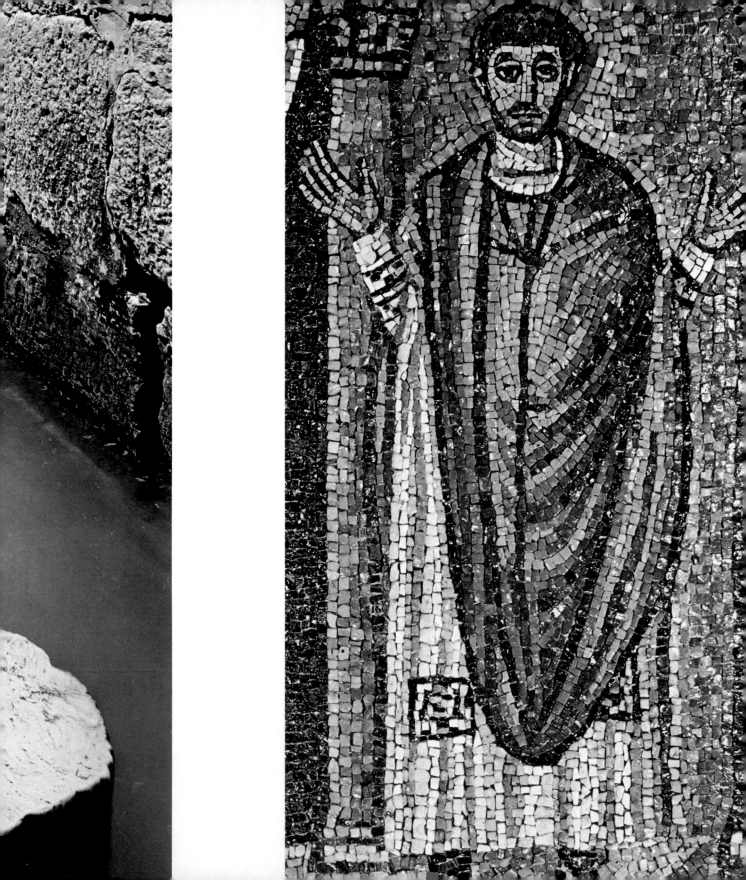

"Whoever believes in me will come to life" (Jn 11:25)

The evangelists tell us repeatedly that people were amazed at Jesus and would ask each other: "What sort of man is this, that even the winds and the sea obey him?" (Mt 8:27). Who is this man who is so different from the scribes? The people were deeply moved by his personality, as they always are by someone in whom word and life are in total harmony. They asked by what authority he spoke and acted. They felt a compelling power go out from him, which not only drew their attention but summoned them to a decision and sought to move them to action in the form of discipleship.

Signs and wonders

There is something puzzling here: People came to him, listened to his preaching, and saw what he did and how he lived; why, then, did they rarely, if ever, grasp his real intentions and passionate concerns? The reason is that they came with their preconceived ideas and expectations, which he had to fulfill. All their questioning and astonishment could not create sufficient openness in them that they would go out of themselves and believe *him*. In addition, those in authority spoke out against Jesus. Sometimes, indeed, the miracle took place: someone saw that his hour had come, dropped everything else, and went off with Jesus. In that moment a man recognized the significance of this Jesus for his own life! At such moments didn't a miracle take place, a miracle in the fullest sense of the word and the really important miracle?

The deeds and words of Jesus did not fit in with the expectations of people and therefore for most of them the question of his identity remained an open one. Many were even inclined to link him with the devil.

For Jesus, however, "signs and wonders" were part of his message and a means of discovering and finding him, that is, of believing in him and, through him, in God. Therefore he always requires faith: "What is needed is trust" or "Everything is possible to a man who trusts" (Mk 5:36 and 9:23).

Jesus requires faith that he, Jesus, has been sent by God to deliver, by word and deed, the message of God's love for men. He demands faith that God speaks through him. Whoever believes him, believes his message; he believes in God as infinite love, believes in the God and Father of Jesus. So doing, he finds his own God and Father. Consequently he sees himself in a new light, for he sees himself as God sees him (cf. 1 Cor 13:12), that is, as loved by God with an infinite love that sustains him, preserves his true life in time and eternity, and brings him to fulfillment through death.

The marriage feast at Cana

Signs and wonders were intended to bring men to faith in Jesus. According to John Jesus performed the "first of his signs" in Cana at a wedding feast. "And his disciples believed in him" (Jn 2:11).

What happened there? There was a celebration that went on for several days. The wine ran out and caused an embarrassing situation that threatened to put an end to the festivities. And in a small village who would ever forget a marriage feast that had turned into a fiasco? The couple would become the laughing stock of the villagers. But Jesus saved the celebration and with it the whole wedding. This is really to say that he helped the newly wedded couple and preserved them from overwhelming ridicule; he made it possible for them to live their life together like everyone else—in joy and happiness! "He has done everything well!" (Mk 7:37).

That is the decisive fact. Wherever he does, everything can change—anxiety to freedom, sorrow to joy, water to wine. He makes the dumb speak and the deaf hear (Mk 7:37). When they encountered him, men experienced the power that was in him and went forth from him and affected their very bodies.

To the believer Jesus himself is the real miracle of God in our world!

The ten lepers

The story of the ten lepers can help us avoid many misunderstandings, foolish expectations, and false questions. According to Luke 17:11-19 ten lepers were cured and sent off to a priest so that he might declare them clean. After that they could return to their families and the society of men. Nine return immediately, but one comes first to Jesus and thanks him. To him Jesus says: "Your faith has been your salvation." Ten were cured, but only this man has achieved salvation! The restoration of his health by Jesus became a sign for him of something further and far more important, for he experienced the saving power and action of God; in Jesus he experienced God.

The multiplication of loaves

Let us turn to the account of the miracle known to us as "the miraculous multiplication of loaves." It can broaden and deepen our understanding, provided we read the text objectively and not in the light of our preconceived ideas. The account is to be found in chapter 6 of John's gospel and is prolonged by the discourse on the Bread of Life; this discourse shows what the real issues are.

Background is provided by the miraculous multiplication of loaves wrought by the

82

prophet Elisha (2 Kings 4:42-44). What Jesus does, however, is far greater and hardly to be compared with Elisha's action. Jesus is, in fact, not a prophet like Elisha or Jonah: "You have a greater than Jonah here" (Mt 12:41). The impossibility of human help in the great need is brought out clearly by the disproportion between the few loaves and fishes and the multitude of people who "numbered about five thousand." After the meal an immense amount was left over, and the people were amazed.

At this point, however, the account of the miracle is not finished; quite the contrary. Only now do we reach the decisive point, as the account turns into an appeal, an exhortation to *believe* in Jesus as savior and giver of life. But what is the crowd interested in, once they have been fed? John tells us that they immediately wanted something for themselves. For, if this man could perform such a miracle, he could obviously do a great deal more. They have their own preconceived ideas and see in this man who has just fed them only someone to grant them their wishes and desires, someone who can and, if need be, must guarantee their life. Consequently they want to force him to be their king. It is really not Jesus himself who impresses them but the idea they have of him; he must play the part they want him to play and become a means to an end.

Here the question must be asked: Who is Jesus *for us*? What does he really mean to us? What is our response when we encounter him? Do we not frequently react just as the people in that crowd did? Could this be one explanation for the stagnation and boredom of our spiritual lives? Unless we move from what we—all of us, probably—want to a genuine listening to Jesus, there's no hope. Only when we take this step do we ask who Jesus wants to be for us and what he has to say to each of us personally.

Jesus reads the intentions of the crowd and withdraws. On the next day he presents himself to them again in order to tell them who he really is and what he wants to be and can be for men. Unsparingly he shows them how his mission differs from what they expect it to be. They are blind, for if they could really see, they would have recognized the divine meaning of his actions. All they want, however, is to have their bellies filled. He challenges them: "You should not be working for perishable food but for food that remains unto life eternal," which I will give you. The implicit supposition is that a man works for all that he needs in order to live. What he can do or accomplish, he must do himself!

A second question therefore arises: "Is it enough just to have our bellies filled? Are 'bread and circuses' enough?" Admittedly, that is already a great deal—but is it everything? Are we satisfied with material prosperity. The same question can be put differently: Do I need God at all? Do I need Jesus? Do I recognize in my heart of hearts that food and drink and such things are not enough, because I am made for infinity, so that only God himself can satisfy me?

A man cannot provide himself with the food for which Jesus exhorts us to work. Instead, God gives it to him through Jesus. The crowd, who are Jews, understand the words "work for" in a typically Jewish way and ask Jesus: What work does God require? What must we do to please God? They expect Jesus to give them a new interpretation of the Mosaic law and to add new burdens and requirements to the old law. But Jesus answers: "This is the work of God: have faith in the One whom he sent." The hearers don't really understand this: he asks them to believe, and they ask him in turn for a sign. What they have in mind is a sign like the sign of the manna in the wilderness. Jesus tells them: My Father gave the manna to your fathers as a sign of his attentiveness and fidelity to Israel. The gift allayed bodily hunger and thus preserved bodily life, but it did not give unqualified "life," that is, eternal life. Jesus himself is the bread which bestowes this eternal life. "No one who comes to me shall ever thirst." He who stands there before them and with whom they speak is himself the bread that gives eternal life—not just after death when the human being has died, but here and now. Through encounter with Jesus man can obtain eternal life, provided he acknowledges Jesus and through him comes to faith.

The discussion with the Jews continues. They reject Jesus' claim and refuse to believe. Their objection: But this is Jesus, the son of Joseph whom we all know! And according to tradition no one will know whence the Messiah comes, for he comes from God.

Our third question: Doesn't this objection of the Jews express the way we often think? We think we know Jesus, but all we really know is a few "facts." We know this or that teaching about him; perhaps we can repeat all the titles given him in the course of the Church's history. Yet he remains a stranger to us; our hearts do not burn within us. We do not challenge his claim to be the bread of life—but is he really bread for us? Does he really do for our souls, for us as human beings, what bread does for our bodily life?

Jesus urges us to listen to the Father. If a man pushes aside all hindrances and lets himself be moved by the Father, he will come to Jesus and believe in him. But in believing in Jesus and coming to know him, he will also come to know the Father, for Jesus will show the believer what God is like; he will reveal God to him as Father.

Earlier Jesus had said: "work!" and thus had demanded effort and activity on man's part. Now he shows the other side of the coin: God, for his part, seeks to move men and draw them to Jesus. The two aspects go together: human effort and being moved by God. How does this movement occur? It occurs when Jesus speaks and man listens. God leads a man away from listening only to himself. The Father "moves" us through the preaching of the Gospel, but also in our daily experiences; he can move us and lead us to Jesus by means of everything that happens to us. In the vulnerable moments of life and in the threat of death, as well as in the exalted moments of life and in hours of happiness we can learn the meaning of life; we can ask and seek—and listen to what Jesus says. If we have the courage to believe, we will experience the truth that he comes from God. Jesus promises to give the believer a share in God's own life: the believer will have life within himself just as Jesus does who draws his life so radically from the Father that only one term can express his relationship to that Father—Son of God. The life Jesus gives is God's gift. As a result, even death takes on a new quality, inasmuch as the believer is now intimately related to the living God.

Faith in Jesus frees a man from fear and anxiety about his life, for the meaning of both his living and his dying are rooted in God. Faith brings "the glorious freedom of the children of God" (Rom 8:21), to which the Christian is called (Gal 5:13). For this freedom is not to be identified with the "freedoms" man chooses for himself, but is a freedom that God gives.

The Eucharistic Bread

Beginning in verse 51 of chapter 6 the words "bread of life" take on a new meaning. Now Jesus is speaking of the "Eucharistic bread": "my flesh . . . my blood." But enough has already been said in the discourse to enable the hearer properly to understand these words of Jesus and not misinterpret them. Any magical misuse has been anticipated and averted, any idea that mere eating is enough. That danger, of course, is not absent even from the practice of the Christian, for he may receive Communion in order to obtain God's favor or to make himself secure against God. Where this attitude holds the field, Communion has become a mere duty, a human "work"; the recipient simply wants God to be satisfied.

Eating this bread presupposes faith in Jesus as the one sent by God, as God's Son. Then Communion becomes the Father's gift and the sign of his unconditional, unqualified love for man in Jesus.

Jesus says: "The bread I will give is my flesh, for the life of the world." He is the man who lives his life wholly for others and spends himself for them. This attitude would lead Jesus later on to accept death on the cross.

The Jews do not understand how this is possible, for they take Jesus' words in a literal, material sense: they are to eat the earthly body that stands before them. Jesus goes on to say that this eating and drinking are of a special kind that establishes an all-embracing communion with him. In fact, the eating and drinking clarifies, in one respect, who and what Jesus is for the believer and what kind of life he has been living. It is the sensible sign of community between Jesus and all for whom he is the way, whom he has helped to find the truth of their own lives, and whom he is leading into eternal life. Anyone who experiences the truth of what Jesus says, and does so in an ever new and deeper way, will also reflect that he too, because of his union with Jesus, can be bread for the life of the world, and will attempt, according to his possibilities and gifts, to become such a bread for others today and in his present circumstances. If he does, he will "grow into" Jesus more fully: he "remains in me, and I in him."

The conclusion of the sermon is a summons to decision.

The raising of Lazarus

The raising of Lazarus (Jn 11), the last (according to John) of the great signs and deeds Jesus worked, is preceded by a conversation. The sisters of Lazarus, Martha and Mary, have sent word to Jesus about his friend's illness. After some delay Jesus finally journeys to Bethany, where Martha comes to meet him. "Lord, if you had been here, my brother would never have died. Even now, I am sure that God will give you whatever you ask of him." Jesus gives the conversation an almost imperceptible, yet highly important turn, and carefully leads Martha to faith in himself as "the resurrection and the life." Martha speaks of death and he answers: *"I am life."* The rest of the conversation clarifies his meaning. Martha says: "I know he [my brother] will rise again in the resurrection on the last day." Jesus answers: *"I am the resurrection and the life."* When Martha hears the word resurrection, her thoughts go to the distant future, but Jesus is talking of the present. Let her find him now and she will find the life that alone determines true resurrection! Whoever believes in him has found in his person resurrection and eternal life, that is, a life which is independent of bodily death.

"Whoever believes in me will never die." Here and now eternal life is to take possession of man and be given him as a gift. This is not to say that the resurrection after death is turned into a myth. No: both resurrections are true, for the hour of resurrection will come, *and* it is already present when a man hears the word of Jesus and believes. The loss or continued possession of transitory earthly life (bodily life and bodily death) is irrelevant for the loss or possession of abiding divine life.

The evangelist wants to make all this clear to us through the sign of the raising Lazarus. The key point is Jesus' question: "Do you believe this?" Jesus asks that question of Martha and thereby of us.

In this context Jesus' prayer (11:41-42) is important, for it shows once again the reason why Jesus can give men this eternal life. At the same time his prayer informs the crowd standing around of the source of his power, his authority, and *his own* life: The Father is the source of it all. Jesus himself is not the origin of it, but he simply does what the Father commissions him to do. He stands in a unique relationship to the Father. This relationship of Jesus to God and to his Father and of the Father to him is not something cut and dried, as it were, not something static. It has nothing to do with the biological order, as though it were a matter of Jesus having been generated in a bodily way by the Father. On the contrary, it is a wholly personal relationship, a vital communion that is being renewed and made real at each moment; thus it is somewhat comparable to the relationship of communion between two human beings.

Once again: This eternal, divine life influences our present bodily life and "rescues" it for eternal life (cf. Jn 4:14). Consequently the believer can say: "To me, 'life' means Christ; hence dying is so much gain" (Phil 1:21).

The raising of Lazarus is a way of manifesting and impressing on the hearer the truth of Jesus and his significance for man's salvation. It is a way of calling the hearer to make a decision, that is, to accept his inescapable responsibility before God and himself.

This Jesus, the Christ, can help even when all human effort and hope, all seeking and struggling, even all despair, are exhausted. Indeed, precisely when man can do no more, when his mortality paralyzes him and no consolation seems possible, when all the idle words and lies have shown their true face and everything—love, goodness, human concern, effort of any kind, suffering and misfortune—seems meaningless, then we see Jesus before us, ready to rescue and lead us to salvation. He confronts us and restores everything: "See, I make all things new" (Rev 21:5). But as of Martha, so of us he asks the question: "Do you believe this?"

The giving of the keys

After the multiplication of the loaves Matthew reports (chapter 16) the scene at Caesarea Philippi in which Jesus gives the keys to Peter. It is to be noted that the incident is located between the demand of the Pharisees for a heavenly sign and Jesus' first prediction of his passion. He had answered the Pharisees that the only sign to be given would be the sign of Jonah, which is an unmistakable reference to the death and resurrection of Jesus. Now he will speak to his disciples of his coming passion. He asks them: "Who do people say that the Son of Man is?" The disciples tell him what they have heard people saying. Then, since he has always set them apart and given them a share in his mission, he asks them what they themselves think of him. Peter answers: "You are the Messiah, the Son of the living God." With this statement that Jesus is Messiah (Christ) and Son of God, Peter becomes the foundation of the Church: His faith is her faith, his confession her confession.

Then Jesus commissions him to take charge, in the Church which is Jesus' community, of the keys to the kingdom of heaven. As Mt 18:18 shows, the commission is not given to Peter alone but to the community as a whole.

Jesus then tells Peter the role that is his in the Messianic age. John 21:16-17 expresses it more clearly: "Feed my sheep!" Peter, like Jesus, is to be leader of the disciples, the community. He is to do so on the basis of a very personal relationship and communion of intimate love for Jesus.

In Luke (22:32) Jesus says to Peter: "I have prayed for you that your faith may never fail. You in turn must strengthen your brothers." Peter later denied Jesus and did not stand "near the cross of Jesus" (Jn 19:25). But he repented, confessed Jesus anew as the Christ of God, and strengthened his brothers by restoring their faith in Jesus after the latter's death when it had been deeply shaken (cf. Mt 26:31).

The pictures on the following pages are of:

46 *Distribution of bread at the "multiplication of the loaves" (ivory, Ravenna)*
47 *Head of Jesus (ivory, Darmstadt)*
48 *Grotto of Pan with source of Jordan near Banijas*
49 *Head of Peter (relief on sarcophagus, Arles)*
50 *Floor of synagogue at Naaran near Jericho*
51 *Jesus raises Lazarus (Greek icon, Athens)*
52 *Lazarus comes from the tomb (Greek icon, Athens)*
53 *Road to Jerusalem and view of the city*

"The hour has come for the Son of Man to be glorified" (Jn 12:23)

Like other Jews, Jesus went up to Jerusalem with his disciples for the celebration of Passover. There are numerous indications that he gave a great deal of thought to the pros and cons for this step. After the many and at times harsh discussions he had with the scribes and Pharisees, and in view of their reactions to him and plots against him, he concluded that he could not avoid a confrontation; everything pointed to this. At first he hesitated, but when it had become clear what the moment required of him, when he recognized that this course of action was the Father's will for him, he went up to Jerusalem after his disciples, but "as if in secret" (Jn 7:1-10). This meant that he was ready to travel his appointed way to the very end and, if need be, die for the mission entrusted to him. Even his disciples, or some of them, must have felt some doubt about whether his course was the right one, as Jn 11:16 indicates, where Thomas resolutely declares: "Let us go along, to die with him."

Entry into Jerusalem

The entry of Jesus into Jerusalem shows us how tense the situation really was. Many of his own followers and the people generally (insofar as they took an interest in him at all) regarded him at this time as the political leader who would liberate them from Roman overlordship and as the future "king of the Jews" who would re-establish the Jewish kingdom. Everywhere he heard the jubilant outcry: "Blessed is the reign of our father David to come" (Mk 11:10).

In Jerusalem itself he was drawn into constant disputes, and the debate with the scribes became even more intense. Finally the Jewish leaders sought to arrest him by some trick or other, so that they might kill him (Mk 14:1). But since they knew that part of the populace was on Jesus' side, they thought it prudent to keep the people ignorant of their plotting. One of the twelve, Judas Iscariot, offered to help them (Mk 14:10).

The supper

Jesus met with his disciples in the "supper room" in order to celebrate the Passover meal, the feast in remembrance of their ancestors' exodus from Egypt and rescue by Yahweh. It was celebrated in the form of a family feast and in accordance with a set ritual. Only unleavened bread was eaten; red wine was drunk. The master of the house spoke the blessing and, in answer to a question from the oldest son, explained the meaning of the actions.

Jesus celebrated this Passover meal with his disciples. In the course of the memorial meal, which his disciples had known from childhood and with the meaning of which they were quite familiar, Jesus took bread, gave thanks, broke it, and gave each disciple a piece of it. As he did, he said: "Take this, it is my body." He also took a cup, spoke the blessing over it, handed it around, and they all drank from it. As he handed it to them he said: "This is my covenant-blood, shed for many" (Mk 14:22-25). The former covenant with God, established at Sinai, was now fulfilled. Jesus' (obedience even to) death establishes the new covenant, with which God replaces the old; this new covenant aims at the salvation of all mankind. Jesus sacrifices his life "for many." This sacrifice, that is, love, is the law of the new covenant. As he breaks bread and distributes it to the twelve who are with him in the supper room, so he distributes his life and his very self. He offers it for them and for all men. Whenever in the future they break bread and eat it in memory of him, they will have a sign of his life and death. As they eat this one bread that is broken and it nourishes them, so he nourishes them, for he has become their life-giving food. That is really what he is! He gives all a share in himself and in this way unites them to one another. All the disciples drink of the one cup, and thus all are united to Jesus and to one another. He, Jesus, unites them to himself and gives a sign of union which they are never to forget.

In the supper we find the fullest expression of what Jesus meant to do, of what he was and is for men, and how closely he binds together those who share in this Communion. The sharer does not receive something he can take and "bury" as though it were purely his own possession; rather, he shares in Jesus himself and allows himself to be caught up into Jesus' involvement with and self-sacrifice for his brothers. In other words: in those who eat this Bread we may recognize and experience the love of Jesus himself as they spend their lives for their brothers.

In this action of his, Jesus tells us, God is entering into a new covenant with mankind. Here we glimpse God's real intentions and see how far he goes in order to win men. (Think of the parable of the prodigal son!) As Jesus hands himself over to men, so too does God, in order to bring all men home to him. In Jesus God reaches out to all who are lost; they are men created after his own image and likeness, and God wants them to find in Jesus reconciliation, peace, and salvation. Whenever and wherever anyone in our world thinks of Jesus and tells others of him, they are to do what Jesus did at the supper: "break bread" and "drink of the cup," in order to make it clear what the real mystery of Jesus is.

It takes no special erudition to understand all this, but it does take a docile heart. When Paul writes: "Every time, then, you eat this bread and drink this cup, you proclaim the death of the Lord until he comes!" (1 Cor 11:26), he is saying that whoever takes part in this meal "proclaims" by that very fact that he has attached himself to Jesus and is united to him; that in Jesus God has revealed to us men his love for us; that we have been accepted by God as his children! He confesses Jesus and makes it clear that he accepts the goal, the program, the life-style of Jesus and will live them in imitation of Jesus. He says that he will do so even though many of his colleagues and acquaintances, many perhaps even in his own family, may have quite a different attitude. Perhaps they smile indulgently at his beliefs. No matter: he will remain united to Jesus and faithful to him, even though this may prevent him from "making something of himself" according to worldly standards.

If a man eats of this Bread, he knows that he is united to all others who eat of it. Don't underestimate the significance of this "knowing"! One individual, by his participation, strengthens his brothers, and this community of brothers in turn strengthens him. To believe in Jesus and to keep his memory as he bade us do is not an affair for isolated individuals (I, all by myself), but for the whole body of those who receive their life from Jesus.

In speaking of the Eucharist (1 Cor 11:27-34) Paul warns us not to eat the Lord's Bread unworthily. He has in mind here not this or that specific sin or disorder, but the basic sin, the one that most fully and properly deserves the name: the lack of love, the egoism that lives at the cost of others (as in the Corinth of the time). You cannot "eat and drink" the love of Jesus and at the same time live in an unloving way! Anyone who desires to take part in the memorial banquet of Jesus and thus have part in Jesus himself, is well aware that he is always "unworthy." Does he not lag far behind Jesus and fall far short of the ideal to which Jesus in his death challenged his followers? But in sharing the meal, he reforms his life (cf. Mk 1:15), believes in the good news, and with all his heart accepts Jesus and the mission Jesus gives him—this in opposition to all the lovelessness and injustice in the world, no matter whence it comes, even if it comes, as it often does, from his own heart.

The washing of the feet

The fourth evangelist, John, has replaced the account of the supper that we find in the other gospels with an account of the washing of feet. Here Jesus gives his disciples an unmistakable sign that will everywhere and always remind them of him: he washes their feet. The sign is to remind them of him and what he has done for them. The special thing about this gesture is that it is their master, Jesus, who does this service for them. That is why Peter objects; he feels there is something wrong here. But when Jesus explains that through this action Peter will have a share in Jesus' heritage, Peter cries: "Lord, then not only my feet, but my hands and head as well" (Jn 13:9). Jesus washes the feet of each of the disciples, so that he may render the same service to each individually and thus give himself to them in a way that says: "I am your servant." In his gesture he sums up the basic meaning of his life, all that he has ever said and done, indeed his life in its entirety. Elsewhere he puts it this way: "Whoever wants to rank first among you must serve the needs of all" (Mk 11:44). He tells his disciples not to seek to be great for their own sake, not to "want to make something of themselves," but rather to be great in the service of others. For themselves they should seek nothing; in positive terms, this means they should seek to be ready to give up everything for the sake of the others so that the latter too may obtain "life," the authentically human, meaningful, free life that is a sharing in the life of God (cf. Mt 20:20-28).

In the washing of the feet Jesus shows his followers what it means, in a specific situation, to be a disciple and love one's neighbor. They will be able to recognize, in the various situations life offers, the possibilities of doing the loving thing and being there for others. The Spirit himself will urge the disciples on to this. Jesus is not concerned with a particular act of charity alone, but with a comprehensive attitude and basic outlook of man to his fellow-men: he is to love them. To love a fellow-man means to accept, in an unconditional way, the man himself and all that is part of him.

Life offers daily opportunities of acting in this way. The task is to see them and "seize" them before they slip away. "To love another means to stand by him when all others reject him; to have time for him when all others pass him by; to rescue him from his confusion and stubborn isolation; to accept him despite his coldness and indifference" (Manfred Hausmann).

Paul exhorts us: "Do not conform yourselves to this age but be transformed by the renewal of your mind, so that you may judge what is God's will, what is good, pleasing and perfect" (Rom 12:2). This is something that has constantly to be put in practice all over again. We have to experience various situations and learn to evaluate them properly. We need imagination, ideas, inventiveness, mutual help and encouragement, alertness and initiative.

"As I have done, so you must do": this is a challenge to the Christian to "learn to value the things that really matter" (Phil 1:10).

In the years immediately ahead, this may well mean that we must bestow special care on those human beings who cannot cope with life in mass society, cannot meet its demands. It may well mean, right now, that we must be concerned for those who cannot cope with illness, neglect, or a rejection of love; who are crushed by loneliness or hide their distress and inner emptiness behind a lot of loud talk. Today, when so many men can only complain and be dissatisfied, the Christian must share what faith in Jesus has bestowed upon him: joy, trust, patience, hope, security!

A few words of the priest Zossima in *The Brothers Karamazov* sum it all up: "Brother's, love the joy of men!"

100

Jesus on Mount Olivet

After the supper Jesus went with his disciples to Mount Olivet as he had often done before. He knows his end is near, and the fear of death grips him. His disciples sleep. Amid the assault upon him he prays: "Father, if it is your will, take this cup from me; yet not my will but yours be done" (Lk 22:42).

His words remind us of the Passover meal at which each guest passed the cup to the next. Jesus would prefer now not to drink of the cup, for it is filled with his rejection by people and leaders and with his repudiation by those among whom he belonged by birth and whom he wanted to lead to salvation; it is filled with suffering. Therefore he prays: "dear Father" (*abba*), let the cup pass me by, let me not have to drink of it.

No matter what comes, however, he trusts his Father. No doubts about God assail him; he is not harrowed by the question whether God can demand such a thing of him or whether he has deserved such a fate and why he is the one who— No! his only concern is do what the Father wants.

What does the Father want of him now? In the "ten words," the Decalogue, it is written that "The Lord is our God, the Lord alone! Therefore, you shall love the Lord, your God, with all your heart" (Deut 6:4-5). It is also written there that a man shall make no image of God for himself, that is, shall not try to tell God how he may act or what he may require. But what does this mean for Jesus in his present situation?

God wants Jesus always and everywhere to stand up for the truth which he was sent to reveal: that God is love. That is the deepest conviction Jesus has; it is so deep and strong in him that he guarantees the truth of it with his life, so deep and strong in fact that he *is* that truth.

He must and will bear witness to this truth against every other conception of reality, even in a situation that means the risk of his life. But in doing so, he is himself and true to himself. The high priests and scribes are determined to get rid of Jesus. Everything goes as planned. God does not intervene, for he is not a *"deus ex machina"* who will rescue Jesus in a "miraculous" way from this situation. But God does strengthen Jesus so that he may go his way to the end. Jesus is ready to meet death. It is in this sense that we are to understand the statement: Because of men's sins he had to suffer this fate, and it was God's will.

Today we often hear it asked: Why did God want the death of Jesus on the cross? Why did he require the blood of this man in order to reconcile men with himself? Wouldn't it have been possible without this kind of "tribute" to God?

Once we properly understand the path Jesus was following and his acceptance of death, we will not ask such questions, for they will be without point. Moreover, such questions betray an idea of God that does not correspond at all to Jesus' idea of God. The God and Father of Jesus Christ is not a threatening demon or a vengeful superman, of whom we would of course try to rid ourselves.

The crucifixion of Jesus

After being taken prisoner Jesus was brought by the Jewish leaders to Pontius Pilate, the governor of the province, for he alone could pronounce a death sentence. How was Pilate to understand what was in the minds of these men? They present Jesus to him as an insurgent; here was an area where Pilate felt at home. Jesus was sentenced to death, then taken out and crucified on the hill of Golgotha as a criminal.

The gospels of Matthew and Mark report one of the last words spoken by the crucified man: "My God, my God, why have you forsaken me?" (Mt 27:46). The words occur in Psalm 22 and are evidently to be taken in the context of that Psalm as a whole. Jesus does not make a prayer only of the second verse! The Psalm speaks of both the suffering and the hope of the just man. Jesus looks upon himself as one of the many who suffer and know fear, whose lives are destroyed by others, whose humanity is crushed. As he had joined them in life, so he joins them in death. On the cross he hangs beside those, too, who have died in despair, cursing men or their own lives. We are given a sign of this, for one of these social "outsiders," hanging there alongside of Jesus, turns to him, and Jesus promises: "I assure you: this day you will be with me in paradise" (Lk 23: 43). Now, at this very moment when your heart is moved, you share in eternal salvation and the kingdom of God is thrown open to you.

Thus, from the cross Jesus shouts out to the world his confidence that even in death God can and will save; dying, he surrenders his life into God's hands with the psalmist's words: "Father, into your hands I commend my spirit" (Lk 23:46; Ps 31:6).

Taking up one's cross

Jesus had told his disciples and the people over and over again that anyone who wished to follow him must take his own cross upon himself (Mt 16:24; Mk 8:34).

Think of all the things this call to true discipleship has been turned into in the course of history! Yet Jesus' words are not telling us that suffering is to be regarded as good, nor are they requiring asceticism and penance for their own sake. On the other hand, there is no looking at the world through rose-colored glasses, no closing of the eyes to the world's reality. Rather, the world, and man in it, are seen as they really are, with all their bodily wretchedness and spiritual distress.

A disciple does not have things easier than other people, his faith does not guarantee him a carefree life, and he does not pray to be free of suffering and distress. In his prayer the disciple of Jesus will always follow the lead given by the life and prayer of his master. This means he need not seek the "cross," for it comes to him from every side; in part, he is his own cross. In desiring and doing what God wants he takes his cross upon himself. Taking up his cross daily means always asking what God wants, but asking with his eyes fixed on Jesus. It means accepting what human life brings without despairing or taking refuge in illness or gossip or alcohol or. . . .

The example of Jesus tells the disciple he must deny himself, set himself aside, in order to do what he knows to be God's will (cf. Rom 12:2). That example challenges the disciple to turn his faith into courageous action and to go his way—like Jesus. As in the life of Jesus, so in the disciple's life the cross and suffering have a different look than they do in other men's. They are no longer meaningless. Jesus wants his disciple to turn away from the questions "Why?" and Why me?" (questions that are indeed natural enough but only wear a man down) and to see in the cross and suffering a challenge and even a mission. He would have his disciple follow him in accordance with words that become fully understandable only when a man does follow Christ: "Did not the Messiah have to undergo all this so as to enter into his glory?" (Lk 24:26), and with confidence that the Father is fully aware of what is happening (cf. Mt 6:8). Then the disciple may not only succeed in saying, with God's servant Job, "The Lord gave and the Lord has taken away"; he may even manage to pray with a liberated heart, "Blessed be the name of the Lord!" (Job 1:21).

Jesus asks his disciple to devote his full energies to changing for the better what can be changed, but to accept and endure what cannot be changed.

The disciple says "Yes" to life in all its reality. How rarely this "Yes" is unreserved and genuine! But to the extent that it is successful, it reveals its liberating power. Because he no longer seeks only himself, the disciple can accept other men and the challenge they represent. The man who travels this road isn't satisfied to meet the suffering of a "stranger" with cheap clichés. He keeps an objective and critical attitude to himself, so that he may the less easily succumb to the self-deception that sees one's own cross and suffering as greater and heavier than that of others or that indulges in self-pity. He is on the watch not to add to the world's suffering and distress, not to increase the burden of others but to help them carry it. The example of Jesus has become a law for him: "Help carry one another's burden" (Gal 6:2).

Saying "Yes" to life

The words of Jesus about carrying the cross are abused when one appeals to them as an excuse for weakness or the inability to face life, for injustice or oppression. Carrying the cross requires courage and the effort of the whole man and all his faculties:

healthy self-awareness, and the determination not to let himself be overcome by the vi-cissitudes of life; the determination to be just and the effort not to let evil be victorious in this world. It requires resisting narrow-mindedness, hypocrisy, boredom, and much else. Jesus loved life and affirmed it without reserve. He was all for joy in life. But with his words on carrying the cross he was challenging his disciple to see life in its totality, with its happiness *and* sorrow, to accept it, and to be patient even when life seems filled with nothing but wretchedness and illness, when it seems blighted, twisted, hopeless, and meaningless. Here is where the true follower proves himself. But in return he is promised: "Whoever holds out till the end will escape death" (Mt 10:22).

Yet how often a man's strength fails! In his pain and despair he cannot think of tomor-row, and is satisfied if he manages to get through today. Perhaps faith—the "knowledge" that the Crucified Christ is close to him—can comfort him and give him strength to face the next hour. But in such a situation may not even the face of the Crucified Christ grow dim? And suppose the last remnant of humanity in a man is broken by severe pain or torture?

When we are confronted thus by the terrifying, annihilating power of the evil one, what are we to do? We can only stammer: "God, be merciful to us sinners," and trust in his compassion for us all. The disciple of Jesus, and the whole Christian community, are bound by Jesus' words on carrying the cross to become the servants of men and to help them bear their burdens as far as possible.

The pictures on the following pages are of:

"He has been raised" (Mt 28:6)

Were Jesus and his cause defeated on the cross? Were his life and work now to be forgotten by the living, because the facts had shown them to be lies? When God did not rescue him from the cross, he seemed to deny him and his message and to reject him as a godless man and a "sinner." But what kind of a God would he be who could reject such a life! If God really did reject Jesus, then all the business about his love for men is nonsense. But then, too, everything becomes hopeless and meaningless.

Meaning of the Easter stories

In the minds of many Christians, the contrast between the message of God's reign, which Jesus preached, and the latter's death on the cross, is very much softened, if not entirely canceled out. The reason is that they know how, after all, things did turn out. But the evangelists, or at least Mark, the first of them, did not thus eliminate the tension. The Easter stories of the New Testament are an answer to the questions the contrast raises, but they do not weaken the impact of the cross in the process. The harshness of death and the agonizing "Ended!" that death stamps upon a human life are not softened into a simple "It was bad, but not hopeless!" Jesus, after all, did not return to just another form of earthly life, nor does he continue his earthly life in another world, somewhere or other; his corpse was not "revitalized." An empty grave, as such, tells us nothing about the person who had been buried in it.

The New Testament does not allow us to look upon death as an innocuous transition in the sense of a self-evident or natural process of some kind: "die and become something new!" What happens rather is that in death all the possibilities known to earthly history or human imagination, indeed all the possibilities open to men, are left far behind and transcended in something totally new.

The New Testament presents the Easter event as a deed possible only to the living God and a new act of creation. In this act God manifests his true power, showing that he is Lord of death and can rescue man even in death. He has raised this Jesus of Nazareth, who was crucified, to new life. And in thus giving Jesus a share in his own eternal life, he acknowledges him and confirms him as the Christ or his own anointed one.

When the risen Christ now "reveals" himself to certain witnesses chosen in advance by God, he acts as witness to the fidelity and truthfulness of God. But he himself no longer belongs to this world; he exists now in eternity, in the definitively real world of the living God. Having experienced his post-Easter revelation of himself, his disciples now confess him to be the Christ of God and the Son of God. They invite other men likewise to acknowledge him and to confess "to the glory of God the Father: Jesus Christ is Lord" (Phil 2:11). In this brief message we have the basis of all Christian hope and all Christian preaching.

The evangelists report that Jesus appeared to the disciples, that they saw him, that angels told them he was alive: "He is not here. He has been raised" (Mt 28:6). God's action and divine reality itself are made manifest, as God shows his Son to be alive and glorified. Jesus "shows himself" to the disciples and encounters them as the living Christ. They experience his presence and his witness to himself as the risen, exalted Messiah. His appearances are a revelation from heaven.

The question of *how* the one who thus appears could be perceived is unimportant to the evangelists; nor do they attempt to depict the resurrection itself. "He appeared to them" is a statement that cannot be further specified or explained in terms of our understanding of human vision. Our ordinary representations are insufficient.

Jesus lives

"Jesus is risen" means that Jesus of Nazareth now lives—the same Jesus in whose presence the disciples had been and with whom they had lived, the same Jesus who on God's behalf laid claim to the lives of men, the same Jesus who died on the cross! He is not an ethereal being or a soul or an angel or anything of that kind. Yet this Jesus does share in the Father's glory. We cannot indeed know what this new man "looks like," because the radical barrier of death cuts off all access to him.—That is what the disciples tell us.

Anyone who objects that this is a pretty big claim to make must ask himself whether it is greater than the claim that God is love, despite all the "impossible" situations we run into in our world, or greater than the claims made for the kingdom of God.

Jesus' preaching is authenticated at that decisive point where death issues its threat to life. For Jesus says: at this moment God approaches man and tells him that he, God, intends to be man's life and everlasting future. The question of the resurrection is then, in the last analysis, a question concerning God and what man believes him capable of. Paul puts it very accurately: "If Christ was not raised, your faith is worthless" (1 Cor 15:14).

Jesus lives by the power of God! But this implies that he now lives with the Father for his disciples and his community. Just as it was for men that he lived his life on earth at a certain time in history, so now he lives for them with the Father. This "for" is not something superadded, something without which he would still have been Jesus of Nazareth. No: it expresses the innermost being and nature of Jesus.

By means of numerous stories the disciples bear witness to their experience of Jesus and invite others to believe in him as the risen Lord.

Emmaus

Luke tells us (24:13-35) of two disciples on the way to Emmaus, a small village near Jerusalem. They were conversing about what had happened. Jesus approached them and journeyed on with them. They did not recognize him for they were too wrapped up in themselves, in the collapse of all the hopes they had set on Jesus, in their sadness and disillusionment. In their eyes, everything was over. They must figure out how to deal with the situation!

Jesus first sought to win their confidence by letting them talk and listening to them. Then he cleared the way to faith for them by using the Old Testament—this for men who were Jews! Now they listened to him. He has turned them away from themselves to the word of God and explained that word to them. When they reached their destination and the stranger (who really wasn't a stranger now) prepared to continue on, they spoke the very kind and compassionate words: "Stay with us. It is nearly evening—the day is practically over" (24:29). He did stay with them. Then, as they were at table, "he took bread, pronounced the blessing, then broke the bread and began to distribute it to them" (24:30). Suddenly everything became clear to them. They knew that gesture—that was the way Jesus did it! Now they knew, "saw," that it was "the Lord"; now they believed that Jesus was indeed alive. "Were not our hearts burning inside us. . . . ?"

Whenever his disciples speak of him, he joins them and is a vital presence among them. When they break bread with one another, he is there. When they serve men and act as he once acted, he lives in their midst, he, "the Lord," is there!

Unbelieving Thomas

John tells us a story about Easter (20:24-29) that is just as well known as the story about the disciples at Emmaus: the story of doubting or unbelieving Thomas.

Thomas, one of the Twelve, laid down conditions under which he would believe that Christ was risen. He says: "I will never believe it without. . . ." Certain definite conditions must be met, then he will believe. It is precisely this that makes Thomas a "sympathetic" figure to us: He wants to believe, but on his own terms. He has no doubt that God can make dead men live; his problem is not with the resurrection in general, but with the resurrection of Jesus! He knew how Jesus had died, and therefore he wants to see the marks of the nails in hands and feet. For Jews generally and for Thomas in particular, death on a cross meant that God had cursed a man, even though the man was Jesus. This was why he had been scandalized at Jesus' death, and that is the reason for his attitude now. He must be able to identify the man raised up as the man who had been crucified. Thomas, then, is really concerned with the meaning of Jesus' death and with the meaning of all human suffering as well. "What meaning can suffering and death have?" he is asking. He feels that we should not too readily and too easily find consolation in the resurrection for the sorrow and pain of the world. He will not let himself be fooled. In the background, then, there is the inescapable question of Jesus' message concerning God's love for man. Does that message really tell the truth about God? What is the meaning of human life in its present form? In the suffering of Jesus Thomas sees his own real problem embodied: Jesus suffered in an unspeakable way, and other men have perhaps even more to endure. Is all that annihilated, as it were, or brushed aside, or forgotten because of the resurrection? The question is a terrifying one for all who really face it. Thomas does face it and becomes the representative of all who are crushed by the burden of suffering that life or other men lay upon them. He asserts his solidarity with Jesus on the cross and demands to see in the risen one the marks of his suffering. For no one, not even God, can simply declare undone what happened on the cross! Thomas wants to see in the risen Christ the crucified Jesus! God must assure him that suffering has a meaning, even if he, Thomas, cannot grasp it. Thus, when Jesus appears to Thomas (and the other disciples) with the marks of his wounds, Thomas cries, "My Lord and my God!" He acknowledges God in the Jesus who bears the marks of his suffering, for the risen Christ is indeed a proof that the suffering of Jesus, and with it the suffering of all men, is taken into and preserved in God. Whatever a man may have to bear, whatever suffering may make of a man, however he gets through—he is safe in the hand of God.

This is not to say that we have the answer to the why and wherefore of suffering. No, that question remains open. But we can live with the question because we believe and are united to Jesus, the one who was crucified and then raised from the dead.

When a man believes, suffering *need* not stunt him or drive him to rebellion and despair or destroy him. Faith can give the courage and strength actively to accept suffering in all its opaqueness and mystery and to bring it under the rule of God (cf. Col 1:24).

If God dealt thus with Jesus of Nazareth and worked thus through him whom the Father now acknowledges as his Christ and his Son, then the disciples are duty-bound to carry on the mission of Jesus, for the Father, through his Son, commissions them to do so. He sends them out to the nations of the earth, so that all men may become disciples of Jesus and children of God, the heavenly Father. They are not to lay burdens on men nor coerce them, but simply to invite them to take their place at the Lord's table, so that his house may be filled (Lk 14:23). It is by serving men, not by trying to exercise power or domination, that the disciples are to awaken faith, hope, and love. They are to speak as Jesus spoke and do what he did; they are to be "other Christs." "As the Father has sent me, so I send you" (Jn 20:23).

The Ascension of Jesus

Luke recounts the Ascension of Jesus in the Acts of the Apostles (1:2 and 9). He begins by going back a bit and speaking once again of the appearances of the risen Christ: "He showed them in many convincing ways that he was alive, appearing to them over the course of forty days and speaking to them about the reign of God" (1:3). The number forty, a symbolic one, expresses the idea that the time in question was determined by God. Then "he was lifted up before their eyes."

Luke pays special attention to the final appearance of Jesus, which culminates in his commission of his disciples as witnesses to him to the ends of the earth, by power received from the Holy Spirit. They, who had been with him on earth, to whom he had communicated his own faith, and to whom he had appeared as the exalted Lord, were to preach their own newly confirmed faith to all men.

Jesus' command permits no delay; there is no time to wait and look up to heaven.

With this commissioning of his disciples Jesus inaugurates a new age, the time of mission, the time of the Church, during which Jesus' community in his name invites all men to enter into the Father's house where they will share in the love and joy of God himself.

Sending of the Spirit

In the gospel of St. John Jesus speaks repeatedly of the Holy Spirit. His words are especially striking in the farewell discourses (chapters 14-15) where he announces that he will shortly be going to his Father. He speaks there of the Spirit of truth whom he, or the Father at his request, will give to his disciples as an advocate (14:16-26). The Spirit will enable them to be witnesses to Jesus before all mankind (15:27).

John 20:22 relates how the risen Jesus breathed upon his disciples and said to them: "Receive the Holy Spirit. If you forgive men's sins, they are forgiven them; if you hold them bound, they are held bound." The forgiveness of sins is the most important gift the disciples are to communicate to men in Jesus' name. At bottom, sin (according to John) is unbelief. In their preaching the disciples will call men to faith in Jesus, and anyone who believes and accepts Jesus will receive forgiveness of his sins; he will turn from the death of sin to life. John can express this by saying: he will come to the love of God.

Spirit of peace

The Spirit of God and Jesus is the Spirit of peace. He turns the disciples of Jesus into a community of peace, a peace that comes from Jesus and is thus, in the last analysis, his gift. What does all that mean?

Our world is under the domination of death and the fear of death. Consciously or (for the most part) unconsciously, man feels threatened by death. He tries to protect himself against death by every possible means. He suppresses his fear and will have nothing to do with the dying; his pursuit of power, possessions, and reputation is a sign of what he is really trying to do. But by the very act of pushing himself to the fore in an often unbridled egoism, he comes into conflict with other men, creates discord, and falls prey to death. But when a man truly believes the power of fear and death over him is broken and the Spirit of peace rules. The man who believes has become a free man. He need not hold on bitterly to his life, for he is in God's hands.

Spirit of freedom

"Where the Spirit of the Lord is, there is freedom" (2 Cor 3:17). Freedom is here to be taken in a very concrete way as freedom from the forces and compulsions that rule this world: whether it be public opinion ("people say . . .") or a naive belief in progress or a fascination with technology and its "drive" to do everything that can possibly be done; whether it be the "drive" to a career and power over men, or the "drive" to achieve lasting acknowledgement from one's fellows. The freedom given by the Spirit is not caprice nor has it anything to do with the various kinds of "emancipation" we read about. It arises out of that strong union with the risen Lord that for the first time makes possible a genuinely free self-dedication, love, and trust.

This Spirit of freedom is to rule in the community of Jesus; the community is to radiate its presence. If it is to do so, the community must make the freedom in question a genuine possibility for its members and help them create its atmosphere in their lives. Conflicts and difficulties of every kind, indeed all that is possible between men, can occur even in this community; what ought to and must distinguish this community from all others is the way in which conflicts and difficulties are resolved, endured, and clarified. The members of this community are ready to help anyone trapped by such a negative spirit to achieve the freedom and fellowship of the children of God.

The vocation of the Christian community, then, is to reflect its Lord, Jesus, in a vital way and by its very existence to cause the true attitudes of men to come to light. But it can all too easily happen that the Christian community may compromise with "this world," settle down comfortably, or drift along in a blind, self-satisfied way. The Spirit of Jesus, however, will be constantly forcing it to take a stand, constantly stirring up unrest and change, so that he may lead it "out of the land of slavery," that, is, all the varied kinds of self-satisfaction and subjection to power and possessions; in short, all subservience to this world.

Do we not see here the way a Christian community of our day must go, a way that will assure it of the future because the way itself is guaranteed by God and bestowed upon the Church as a gift constantly renewed? If the Spirit of Jesus really intends to preserve the community from falling prey to the "spirit of the age" or from getting imprisoned in the past, then he will turn it outward to the world for the world's weal and woe, outward to collaboration in the effort to secure a happy future for all of mankind. Laments about the "evil world" or anxiety in the face of it are hardly suitable means for achieving such a happy future. The mission of the community of Jesus is to understand the hopes and plans of every age, to act as a corrective, and always, in season and out of season, to enter the struggle on man's side and for the sake of man. This community makes the happiness and prosperity, the peace and salvation of men its own concern. It knows how often in its own history it has been guilty, and therefore it will plead with the "Advocate" to bring it renewal.

What is true of the Christian community as a whole is true proportionately of each of its members. The Spirit wants to free the disciples of Jesus from all littleness and narrowness of spirit and heart ("take my poor little virtues from me!": J. Bergmann). He wants them to be sensitive and vulnerable. He wants to open their eyes when they are blind to the world, and, when they are deaf, to teach them to hear the world calling, so that they may respond.

But "this world" isn't fooled. It knows very quickly whether a man is being honest with himself, upright, incorruptible, without guile.

The Spirit can plunge the disciple into doubt and pile up mountains of questions in his path. The disciple should neither repress nor cultivate the doubts and questions, nor be readily satisfied with the often repeated: "That's just something we have to believe!" The Spirit wants to guide him through the doubts and questions, so that he may discover an ever greater God and achieve an ever freer response and an ever more authentic dedication of himself. The Spirit also wants to teach him patience, so that he may endure the heat and burden of the day when all seems lost. The faith of a given Christian community and of the Church at large will be tested by the way it gives its members help and fellowship in such situations.

Pentecost

Luke wants to make the coming of the Spirit vivid, so that it will be impressed on the reader's soul; in this way, too, the meaning of the event will become clear. In numerous details the event of Pentecost reminds us of Jesus' baptism by John. The latter scene marks the beginning of Jesus' public ministry, Pentecost the beginning of the disciples' mission. The Spirit lays hold of and sends both Jesus and the disciples.

The Spirit comes from God and is in no way sensible. The picture of the rushing wind (in Greek "spirit" and "wind" are related terms) suggests something of the way the Spirit works. Whither does the wind rush? It fills the whole house and all who are in it. So the Spirit fills all. He strikes off the shackles of fear and anxiety, breaks through all reserve, and sweeps all with him.

Many of those present break into praise of God's mighty deeds, while others dub it all nonsense and call the disciples madmen, before going back to their everyday business. That had already been the reaction Jesus had met and it is the reaction the disciple of every age meets, for "no pupil outranks his teacher, no slave his master" (Mt 10:24). But the Church and the disciple may be sure that the Lord is with them all days until this world passes away. Whatever may happen, that is their firm foundation, that the source of their confidence: "rejoice in hope, be patient under trial, persevere in prayer" (Rom 12:12).

The Lord is the Spirit

To celebrate Pentecost is to acknowledge the Spirit God has given us, the Spirit of joy, peace, and the freedom of the children of God. He is the Spirit of Jesus and he honors God through Jesus!

"It was for liberty that Christ freed us [in the Spirit]. So stand firm, and do not take on yourself the yoke of slavery a second time" (Gal 5:1).

"Who will separate us from the love of Christ? Trial, or distress, or persecution, or hunger, or nakedness, or danger, or the sword? . . . Yet in all this we are more than conquerors because of him who has loved us. For I am certain that neither death nor life, neither angels nor principalities, neither the present nor the future, nor powers, neither height nor depth nor any other creature, will be able to separate us from the love of God that comes to us in Christ Jesus, our Lord" (Rom 8:35-39).

The pictures on the following pages are of:

69 The Resurrection of Christ (enamel from the Verdun Altar, Klosterneuburg)
70 Angel and women at the empty tomb (golden antependium, Aachen)
71 Christ and disciples at Emmaus (reliquary of Nantouillet)
72 Christ and the unbelieving Thomas (Wilten Chalice, Vienna)
73 Ascension of Christ (enamel from the Verdun Altar, Klosterneuburg)
74 Outpouring of the Holy Spirit (reliquary at Chartres)
75 Christ as ruler of the world (Schnütgenmuseum, Cologne)

The Language of the Pictures

This book attempts in two different ways to paint a portrait of the man who initially was known simply as "the Galilean" and an itinerant preacher. Many of his disciples came to believe that he was the "Messiah" promised to the Israelite people, and, finally, after his death and resurrection, they confessed him as "Jesus, Son of God" and, under this title, preached him to others.

One approach to "Jesus, Son of God" is afforded by this preaching as it took literary form in the gospels. It has been the task of theologians to tell us what is special about the message concerning Jesus and the "new way" offered to mankind.

The second approach is through pictures. It is, however, only another approach to the same Jesus, whose message has been changing the world for over two thousand years and still seeking to change it today through the mediation of the churches.

The importance of proclamation through pictures

It will not surprise us that, next to the theologians, it has been chiefly the artists who have been fascinated by the figure of Jesus down through the centuries since his sacrificial death on the cross. As early as the third century there was, in addition to the gospels and proclamation in word, a proclamation through pictures. And down to the seventeenth century "art" was almost co-extensive with Christian art.

The importance of the visual presentation of Christian themes, and especially of the life of Jesus, for the spread of Christian teaching can hardly be overestimated. We men of today, who live in "the age of the image" and take photography, television, and picture-essays in magazines and newspapers for granted, are in a position to grasp the importance and expressive power of the "language of pictures." At the same time, however, we are also more critical in our judgment of pictures than men as late as a hundred years ago. We ask very pointedly: "Is this picture true?" We want to know whether images of Jesus and his disciples portray them as they really were and really looked in their day, or whether, on the contrary, the images with their Christian themes are simply artistic inventions.

If we attempt to answer the question, "What did Jesus really look like?" by looking solely to the work of painters and sculptors, the very large number of Christian works of art immediately forces us to deal with very varied statements about Jesus and very varied images of him. We see that a simple answer to our question is not possible.

We must face the fact, first of all, that there is no "portrait" of Jesus, any more than there is any authentic written description of him. But does it follow that all the images of Jesus are false? We will put the question to the pictures in this book. We want to inquire into the possibilities and limitations of Christian art, once it has been acknowledged that Christian art cannot furnish us with "portraits" of Jesus and his disciples.

In order to come as close as possible to the real figure of Jesus, we have introduced into the set of pictures in this book not only images produced by artists but two other types of "pictorial documentation" as well: scenes of Palestine, where Jesus lived and worked, and archeological discoveries that date from the time of Jesus but have often been turned up only in recent years.

The witness of terrain and archaeological findings

The land "where his feet stood" (as it is put in a twelfth-century sermon on the Crusade) has not changed essentially in the two thousand years since Jesus walked the earth. The scenes which Erich Lessing photographed for this book on two journeys through Palestine still show us the place in which Jesus lived and which left its mark on his preaching. If we compare the picture of Galilee in the spring (9) or the Galilean landscape by the Sea of Gennesaret (34) near where Jesus preached the Sermon on the Mount, with the wilderness landscapes of Judea, for example, the "Mount of Temptation" (14) or the country around Jericho (21), we are confronted with a sharp contrast. On the one hand, fruitful, flowering Galilee, on the other, the sterile wilderness of Judea. The life of Jesus unfolded in both regions, through which he passed repeatedly in wearisome journeys on foot. And we may surely say that both regions left their mark on Jesus' preaching. The uncompromising harshness of the wilderness is reflected in Jesus' teaching when he sternly criticizes certain Pharisees, when he calls for renunciation, or when his demands in the area of morality often prove even more severe than those of the Jewish law. The happy landscape of Galilee, on the other hand, is mirrored in the humanness of Jesus and in his special partiality for children, the poor, and the sick.

Even today a pilgrimage to the Holy Land is one of the supreme experiences for a Christian who, perhaps after many years of waiting, is privileged to stand "where his feet stood." The pictures of this book capture some of the impressions such a pilgrim would take away with him. Who can fail to be reminded, on seeing the Sea of Gennesaret (18), of the call of the first disciples, or, on seeing the waters storm-tossed (35), of the "Storm at Sea" and the many crossings which the gospels narrate? The sight of a wheat-field or a vineyard in Galilee (32 and 43) will remind the viewer of the many parables and incidents in which there is question of grain and wine, the two basic foods that ever since the "Supper" are at the center of every celebration of the Eucharist. The sight of the various landscapes suddenly brings alive the places in the gospel where we are told: "From there Jesus went. . . ." The road to Jerusalem (37) is no longer an empty set of words. We see the Holy City (53) with the narrow path leading down into the valley of the Kidron and, without any great effort of the imagination, we can see Jesus on his final brief journey. The olive grove at evening with its immensely old trees and the temple wall in the distance (61) must have looked pretty much the same on that Holy Thursday when Jesus was taken prisoner.

This sense of closeness to the "real" Jesus becomes even more intense when we ponder the archeological finds and the ruins of places and buildings from these early times.

Our first picture, of the statue of the mailclad Roman Emperor Augustus (1), already casts a sudden light on the political situation in Galilee and Judea at the time of Jesus' birth. Rome, a world-power, had occupied the country of the Jews. The command of Emperor Augustus set in motion the census which was the cause of Jesus' parents traveling from Nazareth in Galilee to Bethlehem in Judea. Roman utilitarian structures like the aqueduct at Caesarea (2), the presence of Roman soldiers occupying even the holy city Jerusalem, a Roman governor like Pontius Pilate one of whose inscriptions has been found (8)—this whole situation of a land under occupation makes it very clear to us why Israel in the time of Jesus was in ferment, why small-scale revolts against Rome were constantly occurring, and why the people yearned for the "Messiah" who could liberate Israel from foreign overlordship. Even the death of Jesus must be viewed against this political background, for his execution on the cross (a Roman form of execution) came about because the charge leveled against Jesus before Pilate the governor by the supreme council or Sanhedrin, namely that he was seeking kingly power, represented high treason in Roman eyes, and for it the only punishment was death.

The land, too, in which Jesus lived and the places where he stayed are now coming alive for us, through excavation, in a way that would have been unimaginable even a generation ago. The gospel tells us: "He preached in the synagogues of the land," and now we can see the remains of these synagogues (24, 25, 26, 50). We are told: "He had to journey through Samaria," and now we see the columns of the forum at Samaria, which King Herod had built. We gain an entirely new impression of the mighty temple at Jerusalem when we see the huge squared stones of which the wall of King Herod's temple (19) was built.

Many of Jesus' miracles suddenly take on a new aspect when we gaze, for example, at the pools of Bethesda (38) and Siloam (41) at Jerusalem, where by curing the paralytic and the blind man Jesus aroused the indignation of the narrow-minded Pharisees for healing on the sabbath.

The account of the changing of water into wine at the marriage feast of Cana contains the words: "There were at hand six stone water jars" (Jn 3:6). Theologians and historians of antiquity used to have a lot of trouble with this passage. It was long thought that the text of the gospel was corrupt at this point because excavations had uncovered a good deal of pottery but no stone jars. The recent discovery of stone jars (17) confirms the verbal accuracy of the gospel narrative.

When we see the steps leading up to Mt. Zion and the place of the Last Supper or the worn stone pavement in the courtyard of fortress Antonia (66) where Jesus stood accused before Pilate, we are looking at spots where certainly "his feet stood."

But what of the holy places, the Church of the Sepulchre, or the Church over the cave of Christ's birth? Why are there no pictures of places like these which stir memories and arouse veneration for Christ? Have they no place in a "sermon in pictures" concerning "Jesus, Son of God"?

The aim of the pictures is to show as much "reality" as possible, that is, places in which the "historical" Jesus certainly was present. It is from this viewpoint that the pictures thus far mentioned were chosen. The memorials and churches could be, and had to be, excluded, because these buildings, most of them begun only in the third century or later, can tell us nothing of the historical reality of Jesus, however valuable and moving they may be as evidences of the ongoing worship of Jesus. Research has often enough disproved their claim to be evidences of antiquity, although this fact, of course, does not in any way detract from their true value. Take, for example, the "room of the Last Supper." The building dates in fact from the time of the crusaders, and there is no evidence at all that Jesus really ate the Passover meal with his disciples at this spot. The same is true of the tomb of Jesus. The gospel tell us that on Easter morning an angel rolled the stone away from the tomb. The description indicates a so-called roll-grave, that is, a rock chamber which was closed by a round stone slab that was set in a channel and was relatively easy to roll back. Such tombs, belonging to rich Jews of the time of Jesus, have been found near Jerusalem. We show one of them (68) which probably resembles the tomb in which Joseph of Arimathea had the body of Jesus laid. It is hardly possible, however, that there will be any scientific proof that one of the tombs near and beneath the Church of the Sepulchre was in fact the tomb of Jesus.

Let us summarize what the pictures of the terrain and the archeological discoveries have been able to tell us. We have seen landscapes that Jesus too looked on and roads that he walked. We have seen ruins of synagogues and of structures in Jerusalem in which Jesus was certainly present.

We have also shown places where, according to recent research, Jesus probably was. One such is the place of baptism at the Jordan. For a long time a spot in the wilderness valley of the Jordan near Jericho was pointed out as the place where John baptized, but today a more northern location is preferred (13). For scholars, such as the Jewish expert on the New Testament, David Flusser, rightly argue that in the arid desert near Jericho it would have been impossible for large crowds to gather with John. John was a Galilean and it is probable that after receiving his vocation while in the desert, he preached and baptized in Galilee. It is likely that there, too, that other Galilean, Jesus, met him.

We are likewise left with probabilities as to the place where Jesus promised Peter the "keys to the kingdom of heaven" and confirmed him as foundation of the Church. The gospel tells us simply that "Jesus and his disciples set out for the villages around Caesarea Philippi" (Mk 8:27). Did the important conversation perhaps take place near the cave which contains one of the springs of the Jordan (48)? There was an ancient shrine of the god Pan there and scholars consider it quite probable that Jesus would deliberately pick this place with its pagan shrine to ask the all-important question: "Who do you say that I am?" and to receive from Peter the answer: "You are the Messiah, the Son of the living God."

Artistic representations

Early images

The pictures we have been discussing up to this point have a direct connection with the "historical" Jesus. But for images of Jesus and his disciples we must skip down to the third century, for it is only from this time on that we have pictorial representations of the life of Jesus. This means we must accept the fact that we have no "authentic" portrait of Jesus.

How does it happen that in this instance, so important to us Christians, we have no contemporary pictorial images, even though portrait likenesses have come down to us from far earlier times?

There are two reasons for the lack of contemporary representations of Jesus. One is the fact that portraits were painted only of important and wealthy persons. Jesus and his disciples were neither important nor wealthy. The second and far more essential reason is the prohibition of the Mosaic law against images; this meant that believing Jews (such as Jesus and the apostles were) would not allow pictorial representations of themselves or other men. It took several centuries of change before the early Christian community, which had soon spread beyond the boundaries of Judaism, could seek and allow the witness of pictures to take its place alongside the witness of the Scriptures. The beginnings of this early Christian art date from about the third century after Christ.

With an almost seventeen centuries-long tradition of Christian art behind us and and an immense range of examples, it is hard to decide which pictures to choose. Two factors have always left their mark on Christian works of art: the faith of the artist and the period in which the work of art came into existence and by which its formal characteristics were determined. For our pictorial documentation of "Jesus, Son of God," we have therefore limited ourselves to representations which are as close as possible in time to the period of the historical Jesus, since in those pictures the world of Mediterranean antiquity in which Jesus lived is most likely to be still a vital influence.

Roman-early Christian plastic art

Two things strike us when we reflect on Roman-early Christian reliefs, all of which come from stone sarcophagi of the fourth century. On the one hand, they show a clear liking for portraiture, a characteristic of Roman art. On the other, individual features and the effort at portrayal are absent from the representations of Jesus.

When we speak here of portraiture, we do not mean that we have an authentic portrait of Pilate (65) or Peter (49). What the artist has given us is the typical and, to that extent, portrait-like features of a Roman of high rank and the "characteristic head" of a serious, mature man who may well be like the Peter we meet in the gospels and the Acts of the Apostles. In the scene of the "Raising of the Daughter of Jairus" (36) the apostles have very individual features. We see men of the type the stonecutter met everyday in the fourth century, men who would hardly have looked very different in the time of Jesus.

The images of Christ

When we turn to the representations of Jesus on these same sarcophagi (a Jesus whom the artist thought of as the Christ, the risen Lord and Son of God), we observe that Jesus is shown as a young man, far younger than he could have been at the time of the incident depicted. We also observe the lack of individual features.

We asked above why it is that the artist attempts some sort of portrait of Pilate and the apostles but presents Jesus only as a typical handsome young man without any special individuality. The answer is to be found in the situation in which the sculptor worked. He stood in a strict pictorial tradition in which the faces of men (especially officers and soldiers), which naturally lent themselves to portraiture, were familiar subjects, to be handled however in an individual fashion by each sculptor in response to the wishes of the person who commissioned the work.

But the representation of Jesus, the divine founder of a new religion, was something new and unusual for the artist. Since the person to be represented was a divinity, he solved his problem by going back to a familiar model: the ideal type of the youthful god, as embodied in Apollo, and of the young hero. Consequently Jesus before Pilate (64) and at the washing of the feet (58 is shown as a young god; he appears in the same guise as miracle-worker in the house of Jairus (36), as teacher conversing with the disciples (33), and as the "good shepherd" (44). This latter image was also based on the ancient artistic tradition that portrayed the idyllic shepherd who became for early Christianity a symbol of the Redeemer.

In the choice of the young radiant god as the artistic model for the new representation of Jesus Christ we also sense the optimism and alert self-confidence that marked the young religious community of Christians, which after centuries of bloody persecution had now been given the status of official State religion by Emperor Constantine (died 337).

The prohibition of images in the Jewish law was not the only thing that for a long time hindered the development of an image of Christ. In the first two centuries, when the young Church was persecuted and had to go underground, prudence bade Christians to confess Christ pictorially only in secret signs which meant something only to initiated Christians. We are all familiar with the ☧ monogram which is composed of the first two letters of the Greek word Χριστός (i.e., Christ; literally "anointed [one]"). We are probably also familiar with the image of a fish as a symbol and secret password. The Greek word for "fish" is Ἰχθύς ; the letters that make up the word are the initials in a short profession of faith: Ἰησοῦς Χριστὸς Θεοῦ Υἱὸς Σωτήρ , i.e., Jesus Christ, God's Son (and) Saviour.

Now, given that the community represented Jesus in the traditional form of the youthful god of the ancients and made no attempt to portray him in a "natural" way and with individual features, have we the right to say that this image of Christ is "false" because it does not correspond to historical reality?

If we reflect we will quickly realize that this question would have been meaningless to the early Christians. Their artistic concern was not with the "historical" Jesus who is of such interest to us today. They wanted rather to create a suitable representation of the Christ in whom they believed: the risen Lord, the Redeemer, the preacher of a religion of authentic humanity and brotherhood. Early Christianity found no representation that was better and more appropriate than that of the youthful god. It was an image that expressed their belief and their emotional attitude to Christ. For this reason it was an image of Jesus that was correct from the spiritual viewpoint. As we consider the following pictures we will see how the image of Christ changed with the changing spiritual outlook of the community. We will also come to realize that any representation of Jesus is valid and true if it is the expression of a spiritual attitude of faith.

Byzantine-Eastern art

Roman-early Christian sculpture derived the forms that it developed from the broad stream of the Greco-Hellenistic artistic tradition. The second type of early Christian art, the Byzantine-Eastern, to which we now turn, is also in continuity with Greek antiquity.

The area in which Byzantine art predominated had its vital center in Constantinople or Byzantium, the capital of the Eastern Roman Empire. It became the decisive intermediary in passing on the highly developed artistic forms and techniques of late antiquity to Western Europe; the wealth and variety of the artistic forms it itself developed became a stimulus and model for the Christian art of the West.

If we examine the figures on the alabaster columns which probably originated in fifth-century Syria and today support the baldacchino over the high altar in St. Mark's Cathedral at Venice (6, 20, 63), we recognize in the natural movements, the free flow of the folds in the garments, and the expressiveness of the faces the living influence of ancient Greek artistic forms. It is to the latter that the world owes the first natural representations of the human body and the correct observations of the interplay of muscles and joints that characterizes the movements of the living body. At the same time, however, we find something, for example in the head of the weeping Peter (63), that would not have been possible in classical antiquity and was something new in art: the effort to express the individual. We encounter here a fundamental problem of all art, since it is the aim of art to use pictorial means in order to express the psychic, the emotional, and even the "miraculous."

This effort, which is especially characteristic of Christian art, also confronts us with the special problem of all Christian art. Can art represent "miracle?" Can it lay hold of the "divine" by pictorial means? Is art not more likely to represent Jesus entering Jerusalem on an ass (54) as a peasant riding wearily home from the fields at evening?

Christian artists have always been aware of the paradox of having to use earthly means for expressing what is heavenly and suprasensible. In the Byzantine period this paradox led to the "image controversy" which lasted over a hundred years (726-843) and gave rise to repeated "image-breaking." The central issue in the iconoclastic struggle was whether the veneration of images was to be regarded as idolatry (as the opponents of representational art claimed) or whether the images of Jesus, the Mother of God, and the saints were to be regarded as probative arguments for the effective presence of the events in the history of salvation.

This conception of the probative power of the images of the saints never took hold in the West. Behind it lies an old Byzantine legend that the first images of Jesus, Mary, and the apostles were "not made by human hands" but brought to earth by angels. Other traditions attribute the first image of Mary to St. Luke the evangelist; for this reason the Middle Ages chose him as patron of artists (St. Luke's Guilds). An image of Mary from the hand of Luke (and the world where Byzantine art held sway, from the Balkans to Russia, believed there was such an image) was certainly to be regarded as the embodiment of a presence.

The same conviction explains another characteristic of Byzantine art: its inflexible adherence to artistic forms once they had been elaborated. Western art shows a clear stylistic development: a Romanesque image of Mary is quite different from a Gothic or Baroque image. Byzantine art shows no such development. An icon of Jesus from the sixth century differs hardly at all from an icon of the sixteenth or nineteenth century. For this reason, in selecting pictures to present Byzantine art, we have been able to use images

146

of the twelfth or seventeenth century and still describe them as "early" art.

If Byzantine art is relatively unchanging in comparison with the developing art of western Europe, this attitude is not to be confused with self-satisfaction. Byzantine art too produced a wide range of works in its effort to achieve valid forms that would adequately depict sacred figures and events. It is to Byzantine art that we owe the development of the image of Christ as a bearded mature man, the image, in fact, which came to be regarded as *the* image of Christ. Compare the pictures of the young Jesus (6), of Jesus driving the money-changers from the temple (20), or of the mosaic representation of Jesus curing the blind man (40) with the icon of Jesus (15) or the ivory-relief head of Jesus (47), and we will see how, when the artist turned away from the representation of Jesus as a handsome young god (an inheritance from antiquity), he developed a type of representation which did greater justice to the "teacher," the "friend of men," and the "Lord of heaven and earth."

The creation of a "more correct" image of Jesus was accompanied by an effort at greater expressiveness. The Jesus of the icon gazes out at us with a timeless gravity (15). In the ivory head (47), part of a scene of healing (13), we feel the intense concentration of energy that forces the demon to leave the possessed man. The same expression of concentration is to be found in the three miniatures depicting the healing of sick people (28, 29, 30). All three pictures show "miracles," and in all three the "power" that works the miracles flows out from the face and gaze of Jesus. It is as though the gaze, which is not directed to the sick person, is trying to enter into contact with the Father in heaven in order to effect the cure with his help. The gestures of the hand, which is kept very close to the body, especially in the cure of the paralytic (30), seem almost constrained. But this only helps make it all the more clear that something "spiritual" is occurring here and that the miracle is something beyond comprehension.

But the other type of expressiveness that concentrates everything in the gesture is also to be found in Byzantine art. What controlled and compelling power is in the hand that Jesus stretches out to the tomb of Lazarus (27), who has already been dead for four days! The words of Jesus, "Lazarus, come out!" become here a confirmation of his gesture. The miracle itself has been worked by the hand with its concentration of divine power that compels Lazarus to return to life.

The danger that always lies in wait for religious art, of so representing the incomprehensible (holiness or a miracle) as to make it only too conceivable and to allow the sensible-corporeal form to dominate the element of the suprasensible is countered in Byzantine art by a deliberate playing down of corporeality. The play of the limbs, so masterfully depicted in classical art, becomes more jejune and is concealed by the folds of the garments, because it has become unimportant in comparison with the concentrated expressiveness of a face or a gaze or a gesture of the hand. To the extent, moreover, that Byzantine art sets the sacred figures before a glimmering, wholly unspatial background in mosaics, miniatures, and enamels with a gold background, the element of corporeality is even further reduced. The figures seem to exist in the golden ambiance of an eternity that eludes the mind's grasp.

Medieval art of the goldsmith

The mosaic, in which the art of imperial Byzantium achieves probably its most spendid successes, was not taken over and developed in the West, but the other techniques elaborated by Byzantine-Eastern artists—book illustration, frescoes, ivory carving, and the techniques of working gold—were all taken over by western artists and used in the development of independent forms. It is significant that in this takeover of Mediterranean forms and techniques the German artists north of the Alps achieved their greatest successes in the art of working gold.

Undoubtedly, the Byzantine artists' idea of using shimmering gold in order to abstract the sacred figures from any earthly ambiance was also familiar to artists north of the Alps. In addition, however, there was a typical shift of attitude toward "Jesus, Son of God": for these young and martial peoples he became Christ the King. A king, however, deserved that most precious of materials, gold, in which the power and wealth of a lord, be he earthly or heavenly, was manifested. Consequently, for the German, gold, gleaming enamel, and precious stones were the materials best suited for depicting the person and actions of heaven's king in all their incomprehensibility. To supply such costly materials for the service and glorification of Christ the King was also, in the Germanic view, something that did honor to the human being who commissioned a work.

Precisely because deep faith and pictorial media were harmonized in the work of the early medieval goldsmith to a degree we will hardly meet again at any later period, we have chosen pictures of their work to illustrate the most important part of the "life" of Jesus: the events of Eastertide. It is here that the Jesus of history is transformed into the Christ of faith; without that change Christianity and its spread throughout the world would not have been possible.

The work of these men also reflects once again the evolutionary process peculiar to Christian art: its closeness to nature, on the one hand, and its effort to transcend corporeality, on the other.

The chased gold relief of Mary Madgalene's meeting with the angel at the tomb (70) is very close to antique art from the formal standpoint. The limbs are carefully modelled, the tomb resembles an ancient mausoleum. The gold and enamel panels by Nicholas of Verdun on the Klosterneuburg Altar (69, 73) with their masterful treatment of faces, clothing, and bodies are inconceivable without models from antiquity and early Christianity. The situation is quite different in the panel depicting "Jesus and the Disciples

148

at Emmaus" (71). Here the older model is obscured, for decorative motifs (a stylistic element in Germanic art) cover the gold background which at an earlier period would have been left a bare gleaming surface so that the figures would have seemed almost disembodied. In this work, moreover, the figures convey a new sense of movement that had been unknown in antiquity. Here we have an anticipation of the great western style, the Gothic, and a new sense of the body that owes nothing to antiquity. The scene depicting the unbelieving Thomas (72), though constrained within the limitations of the metal surface, exemplifies the same new style in which, a thousand years after the decline of Greek art, the beauty of bodily movement once more comes into its own.

What mastery of conception, what delight in precious materials, what rich ornamentation we find in the representation of the outpouring of the Holy Spirit on Pentecost (74)! Here once again western art has liberated itself completely from ancient models and created something of its own in a convincing representation of a salvific act of Christ the Lord. For the early medieval art of the west Christ was almost always "Christ the King," and is shown wearing the royal crown (even on the cross) or sits enthroned as Lord of Heaven, as in our final picture (75). Here he sits on the rainbow throne of heaven, holding the book of the gospels, his good news for the world down to our own time.

We have come to the end of our meditation on the pictures that were meant to shed light on the figure of "Jesus, Son of God." But could a "Life of Jesus in Pictures" really have this effect?

In discussing forms of early Christian art we saw both the possibilities and limitations of all Christian art. One of its possibilities at every period is to create the "correct" image of Jesus for that age with its characteristic spiritual outlook. Thus we have the "young god," "the man Jesus," and "Christ the King." We have seen the development of ancient traditions, the invention of new forms, and the stubborn repetition of images, once they had been satisfactorily elaborated, that were intended as efficacious witnesses to the unseen.

As for the limitations of Christian art, we saw, for one thing, the fact that art cannot give us an "authentic" portrait of the historical Jesus and, for another, the ever-present danger of using bodily forms to make inconceivable spiritual realities only too comprehensible and of thus turning religious art into religious trash. If the images presented in the photographs of this book have not succumbed to this danger, the reason is that in them artistic ability and genuine belief in the realities being represented are still united. In these images, therefore, "Jesus, Son of God" comes before us as he really is: true man and true God.

Notes on the Pictures

1 Statue of Augustus on the wall of the stage of the Roman theater at Orange. First century A.D.; 11.65 feet high. The statue of the mail-clad figure was restored in 1951 by piecing together numerous fragments. Original head lost, replaced by a modern copy of another head of Augustus.

2 Two aqueducts supplied Caesarea, Roman administrative capital of Judea, with water from Mt. Carmel, ten miles away. Recent excavations at Caesarea have shown that the foundation of the eastern aqueduct was laid at the period when King Herod founded Caesarea, or a little later, while the western aqueduct (shown in this photograph) is somewhat more recent. For technical reasons this later aqueduct was to a greater extent built on to the earlier one, so that atop the heavy arches the two covered channels run side by side.

3 On the road to Bethlehem. The name of the city, which is situated on a 2,568 foot high hill, means "house of bread" and alludes to the agricultural wealth of the area.

4 Birth of Christ. Early Christian or Byzantine marble relief, 33.93 inches high, 32.76 inches wide. Byzantine Museum, Athens.

5 Recent excavations in the old city at Jerusalem uncovered a stuccoed slab with an incised drawing of a seven-branched candlestick (menorah), 7.8 inches high. What makes this find remarkable is, first, the location of the slab in the "upper city," only 885 feet from the hill of the temple and, second, the certainty that it dates from the time of Herod. We are justified in thinking that the drawing represents the candelabrum in the Herodian temple. If this be the case, we have here the oldest representation of this cult object. Representations of the menorah from the period before, during, and after the time of Jesus are very rare; the best known is the one in the relief on the Arch of Titus in Rome (after 70 A.D.).

6 Disciple of Jesus. Relief from the front left column supporting the baldacchino over the high altar in St. Mark's, Venice. Made of alabaster, the column is 9.75 feet high. The four columns were brought to Venice by the crusaders, probably in 1204. The front two columns were probably the products of the Eastern Church during the fifth century; the back two are perhaps Venetian copies made during the Middle Ages. The inscriptions are medieval and were added in Venice. The figures stand in niches ornamented with shells and divided by miniature columns; they show scenes from the New Testament; the life of Mary, beginning with her birth; the life of Jesus, including his birth, miracles, passion, and ascension. Carved by at least two sculptors, the front two columns are of superior quality.

7 Emperor Tiberius. Gem of blue glasspaste, 2.3 inches high, 1.8 inches wide. The work, dating from early in the reign of Tiberius, is by the gem-cutter Herophilos (son of Dioskurides), who was active from the late Augustan period on. The stone is usually taken as representing Tiberius, although Vollenweider thinks it portrays Augustus. In the Kunsthistorisches Museum at Vienna.

8 Inscription in stone, relating to Pontius Pilate. The text reads: "Tiberieum . . . Pontius Pilatus . . .praefectus Iudaeae," which means: "Pontius Pilate, prefect of Judea, erected a building in honor of Emperor Tiberius." The inscription, found by Italian excavators at Caesarea, is the only non-literary source we have that refers by name to the Pontius Pilate of the New Testament. In the Israel Museum at Jerusalem.

9 Galilee in the springtime. The blooming countryside north of the Sea of Galilee along the road to Safed shows how different this fruitful region is from bare and desert-like Judea.

13 The place of Jesus' baptism in the Jordan has not been established with certainty. Contemporary research has shifted the locale of John's activity from the wilderness valley of the Jordan near Jericho, where it is hardly likely that sizable crowds would gather, to Galilee and the area where the Jordan empties into the sea. The picture shows this spot.

10 John the Baptist. Ivory panel on the chair of Archbishop Maximian (546-56) of Ravenna. The panel is on the front of the chair which is entirely covered by similar panels. The chair is 58.5 inches tall, 23.6 inches wide; the carving, 9.8 inches high, 4.9 inches wide. Place of origin disputed: Ravenna, Egypt, Constantinople? In the Archiespiscopal Museum at Ravenna.

14 Mount of Temptation in the wilderness of Judea, west of the Jordan valley.

11 Wilderness of Judea between Jerusalem and Jericho.

15 Jesus. Detail from an icon of the mid-seventeenth century; painted and signed by Emmanuel Lombardos (active between 1593 and 1647); 11.1 inches high, 12.1 inches wide. In the Paul Canellopoulos collection at Athens.

12 Baptism of Jesus. Icon from mid-seventeenth century, 16 inches high, 12 inches wide. In the Paul Canellopoulos collection at Athens.

16 In the heart of Galilee, 6.2 miles east of Nazareth, stands Mt. Tabor, 1864 feet high, which is regarded as the site of Christ's transfiguration. The picture shows the view from Belvoir, the crusader fortress.

17 Stone jars of various shapes and sizes seem to have been popular in the Judea of Herod's time if we may judge by finds at Jerusalem, Masada, and Qumran. As receptacles for liquids they may have served many purposes. The two jars shown here, both from Jerusalem, are notable for the elegant line of lip and foot.

21 The eroded countryside between Jerusalem and the valley of the Jordan, shown here in the neighborhood of Ain Duk, has a characteristic red coloring in rock and earth, due to oxidation of the iron present. Because of the color the Bible also calls the area "the steps of blood."

18 Sunrise on the west bank of the Sea of Galilee near Bethsaida where Peter and Andrew lived.

22 The Samaritan woman at the well. Details from an icon of the late sixteenth century; 15 inches high, 18.7 inches wide. In the Paul Canellopoulos collection at Athens.

19 A section of the Weeping Wall, that is, the retaining wall on the west side of the temple precinct. The foundation of the spacious temple-terrace required extensive land-fill operations and retaining walls on three sides of the precipitous hill on which the temple stood. The lower sections of these walls, now largely covered with earth, have lasted to the present time despite ravages and repairs. That fact is not surprising when we consider the colossal size of the blocks of stone. The block used in the Herodian temple is on the average from 8.9 feet to 14.8 feet long and from 35.7 inches to 47.25 inches high; the largest is 20.7 feet by 5.9 feet. Typical masonry of this period shows a flat surface with a narrow lip around the edge.

23 Remains of a stately colonnade in the Roman forum of Sebaste (Samaria). The tall, clearly defined bases of the columns show that the latter are to be assigned to the late second century A.D. at the earliest, and probably to the period of the emperor Septimius Severus (193-211), but the original foundations of the forum with its basilica-like central hall date from the Herodian or even the pre-Herodian period.

24 Its splendid location on the Sea of Gennesaret and its rich architectural decor explain the reputation of the synagogue at Capernaum as the most beautiful in the Holy Land. The decor shows beyond doubt that the building was erected in the late second or early third century A.D. However, the frequent mention in the New Testament of a synagogue at Capernaum shows that there had been an earlier building in the time of Jesus. Moreover, one surprising text in Luke (7:5) tells us that this earlier synagogue had been built by a high-ranking officer in the Roman army: "He loves our people and even built our synagogue for us." The view in the photograph is from the stairway through a door in the north side into the main room with its benches along the side wall. The walls were certainly stuccoed and may have been painted as well.

20 Driving of the money-changers from the temple at Jerusalem. Alabaster relief from the front left column of the baldacchino over the main altar in St. Mark's, Venice. Cf. note on picture no. 6.

25 Detail from a pavement mosaic of the later fourth century A.D. in the synagogue of Hammath, near Tiberias, a rabbinical center in Roman and Byzantine times. Probably the most popular motif in the Palestinian synagogues of the Byzantine period (fourth to sixth centuries) was the representation of the interior of a synagogue as symbolized by the sacred objects found therein: the Torah shrine (with columns and gable, coffered door, and curtain), flanked by immense seven-branched candelabra (only partially visible in this photograph) and surrounded by shofar (ram's horn), censer, and lulav (bundle of branches). — Under this structure are the remains of the foundation of an earlier synagogue.

26 The ruins of the synagogue at Arbel. This building, situated west of the Sea of Gennesaret, was an early Galilean synagogue that followed a basilican plan (late second to fourth century, A.D.), like the synagogue of Capernaum, Baram, and Chorazin. Like that of Chorazin, the synagogue at Arbel was built of local basalt stone.

27 Hand of Jesus extended in blessing. Detail from an icon, "The Raising of Lazarus"; early sixteenth century, 11.5 inches high, 12.1 inches wide. In the Paul Canellopoulos collection at Athens.

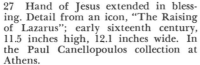

28 Cure of a blind man. Miniature from an evangelistary which contains three full-page portraits of the evangelists and twenty scenes scattered throughout the text. Second half of the twelfth century, from the monastery of Iberon on Mt. Athos; 8.4 inches high, 5.85 inches wide. In the National Library at Athens, Cod. 93.

29 Cure of a leper. Miniature. Cf. note on picture no. 28.

30 Cure of a paralytic. Miniature. Cf. note on picture no. 28.

31 Cure of a possessed man. Detail from an ivory panel that depicts the expulsion of demons in the country of the Gadarenes or at Gerasa; on this occasion the demons left the man and entered into a herd of swine. — Carved at Milan or Reichenau (?), eleventh century; 4.99 inches high, 4.6 inches wide. In the Hessisches Landmuseum at Darmstadt, No. 764.

32 Wheatfield in Galilee.

33 Christ with two apostles. Detail of a relief carved from Carrara marble on the "Sarcophagus of the Miraculous Spring." The scene is the prediction of Peter's denial. Date: about 330. The sarcophagus is 86.2 inches long, 23 inches high, 7.8 inches deep. In the Musée Lapidaire d'Art Chrétien at Arles, Inv. No. 19.

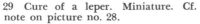

34 The Mount of the Beatitudes near Tabgha and Bethsaida, with a view of the northern part of the Sea of Gennesaret. The area is closely linked with the life and activity of Jesus, for according to tradition the multiplication of the loaves also took place here.

38 The pool of Bethesda lay north of the temple precinct in a suburb of Jerusalem that was built under King Agrippa I (41-44 A.D.), if not earlier. The spacious double pool, important as a reservoir for Jerusalem which had little water of its own, was surrounded in Roman times by columned porticoes, as the ruins indicate.

35 "The Storm at Sea." Eastern shore of the Sea of Gennesaret.

39 Cure of a paralytic. Detail from a relief on an ivory pyxis (the other representation is of the raising of Lazarus). Byzantine work of the fifth century; 3.2 inches high; diameter of pyxis, 4.5 inches. In the Hübsch Collection, No. 1, of the Hessisches Landmuseum at Darmstadt.

36 Raising of Jairus' daughter. Marble relief on the sarcophagus called "Apostles in Pain." Right side of a fragment belonging to the front of a single-zoned coverless "frieze"-sarcophagus; length (reconstructed), 88.14 inches; height, 27.3 inches; depth, 4.29 inches. First quarter of fourth century. In the Musée Lapidaire d'Art Chrétien at Arles, Inv. No. 18.

40 Cure of a blind man. Detail from a mosaic on the north wall of S. Apollinare Nuovo at Ravenna. This is the fourth picture of twenty-six on the life of Jesus; they stand on the walls of the nave, over the windows, at a height of 38.37 feet. Date: about 530.

37 The Roman road from Jericho in the Jordan valley (about 902 feet below sea level) to Jerusalem (about 2703 feet above sea level) was about 16.75 miles long and ascended about 3600 feet. Like the other provinces of the Roman Empire, Judea-Palestine was crisscrossed by roads that served the army as well as business and general traffic. The Romans were the first to build roads (in the modern sense of the term) in Palestine. These roads were built in the period from Nero to Septimius Severus, the high point of their development coming in the reign of the Emperor Hadrian when the Jericho-Jerusalem road was built (about 130 A.D.).

41 The pool of Siloam was built about 700 B.C. by Hezekiah, King of Judah (715-687/686) in order to assure Jerusalem of water during the expected attack by the Assyrians. In order to make the spring of Gihon (outside the city walls) inaccessible to the besiegers, Hezekiah had it blocked up and a tunnel of over 1770 feet built to bring the water into the pool of Siloam within the city. To commemorate this extraordinary technological achievement the King had a (Hebrew) inscription placed on the tunnel wall not far from the pool of Siloam. The inscription is now in the Archeological Museum at Istanbul.

42 A Pharisee. Detail from a mosaic depicting the story of the Pharisee and the tax-collector. This picture is the eighth scene on the northern wall of the nave in S. Apollinare Nuovo at Ravenna. Cf. note on picture no. 40.

43 Vineyard.

44 The Good Shepherd. Relief in Carrara marble on the "Sarcophagus of the Good Shepherd" (incompletely preserved). Date: about 330; length (incomplete), 42.9 inches; height (incomplete), 19.1 inches; depth, 3.9 inches. In the Musée Lapidaire d'Art Chrétien at Arles, Inv. No. 31.

45 Eastern shore of Lake Tiberias, north of Ein Gev.

46 Miraculous multiplication of loaves. Ivory relief on back of chair of Archbishop Maximian; 8.27 inches high, 4.9 inches wide. Cf. note on picture no. 10.

47 Head of Jesus. Ivory relief; detail from cure of a possessed person. Cf. note on picture no. 31.

48 Grotto of Pan. The Paneion (Banijas), near Caesarea Philippi (at the foot of Mt. Hermon, the present Golan Heights), was one of the numerous pagan shrines in the Holy Land; most of these were in non-Jewish areas of the Herodian kingdom. As the name shows, this spot (in an area whose springs feed the Jordan) was a shrine of the Greek nature-god Pan, who, together with the fountain nymphs and with "Echo," was worshipped here until the fourth century A.D. The only remains of the shrine today are the niches in the rocks and the votive inscriptions in Greek. The grotto is mentioned by Flavius Josephus, the Talmud, and Eusebius (fourth century A.D.).

49 Head of Peter. Relief in Carrara marble on the "Sarcophagus of the Giving of the Keys." Detail from the washing of the feet. Date: about 400; 87.4 inches long, 28.1 inches high, 20.3 inches deep (incomplete). In the Musée Lapidaire d'Art Chrétien at Arles, Inv. No. 17.

50 The synagogue of Naaran (Arabic: Ain Duk) near Jericho is a late type of synagogue, represented by numerous buildings in the Holy Land from the fourth to the sixth centuries A.D. The chief characteristic of the type is the presence of pavement mosaics which make use of various decorative motifs. The rich mosaic at Naaran contains, for example, the zodiac, Daniel in the lions' den, and the Torah shrine flanked by seven-branched candelabra. The photograph shows an as yet uninterpreted heraldic group of two gazelles on either side of a tree. The synagogue at Naaran was built in the fifth century.

51 Jesus raises Lazarus. Detail from an icon of the mid-seventeenth century; 20.3 inches high, 16.8 inches wide. In the Paul Canellopoulos collection at Athens.

52 Lazarus comes out of the tomb. Detail from an icon. Cf. note on picture no. 51.

53 The road to Jerusalem descends from the Mount of Olives into the Kidron valley and then climbs up to the hill of the temple. The photo shows, in the distance, the "Golden Gate" in the east wall of the temple; through it, according to tradition, Jesus entered the city. The gate was for this reason later walled up by the conquering Arabs.

54 Entry of Jesus into Jerusalem. Ivory relief on back of chair of Archbishop Maximian; 9.75 or 8.5 inches high, 4.7 inches wide. Cf. note on picture no. 10.

55 The Supreme Council. Detail from a mosaic depicting the examination of Jesus by the Sanhedrin. This is the fifth scene on the south wall of the nave in S. Apollinare Nuovo at Ravenna. Cf. note on picture no. 40.

56 The "pieces of silver." A bronze pyxis with nine Tyrian and three Jewish shekels. In the Israel Museum at Jerusalem.

57 These stone steps near the little church of St. Peter in Gallicantu (a cock-crow), which commemorates St. Peter's betrayal, lead from Mt. Zion down into the valley of the Kidron. It is supposed that Jesus climbed up and down these steps several times on the night of the Last Supper which he probably celebrated in a building on Mt. Zion.

58 Jesus washes Peter's feet. Relief on the "Sarcophagus of the Giving of the Keys." Cf. note on picture no. 49.

59 Jesus and St. John. Detail from a miniature depicting the Last Supper. Cf. note on picture no. 28.

60 Cup of suffering. Of the metal industry which we know from literary sources to have existed in the Herodian period we have but scant remains in the form of emblems and coins, lamps and ossuaries from Jewish graves around Jerusalem. This photo of part of an ossuary shows a cup-shaped metal container with two high curved handles, standing between two rosettes. The tall foot as well as the upper part of the vessel (between the two handles) are so amateurish in comparison with the sure lines of the rosettes that the vessel is thought to have been a later addition by the son of the deceased man, who wanted to give his father an image of a Jewish vessel for temple or festive use to take with him into the next life. Israel Department of Antiquities, Jerusalem.

61 In the Garden of Gethsemane, on the western slope of the Kidron valley, some very old olive trees still stand. In the background can be seen the eastern wall of the temple height.

62 Jesus before the high priest. Detail from a miniature in an evangelistary. Cf. note on picture no. 28.

63 Peter repentant. Detail from an alabaster relief on the front right column of the baldacchino over the high altar of St. Mark's in Venice. Cf. note on picture no. 6.

64 Jesus and a Roman soldier. Detail from a relief depicting Jesus before Pilate, on the "Sarcophagus of the Giving of the Keys." Cf. note on picture no. 49.

65 Pilate. Detail from same relief as in no. 64.

66 The place of judgment where Pilate sentenced Jesus is located by many scholars in the citadel on the west wall. Others, however, especially the foremost authority on Jerusalem, Fr. L.-H. Vincent, O.P., of the Ecole Biblique in Jerusalem, locate it in the fortress Antonia which according to the traditional view, generally accepted today, was at the northwest corner of the temple precinct. And in fact Fr. Vincent has found in that area a pavement (Greek: *lithostratos*; Aramaic: *gabbatha*; i.e., stone pavement) which can with high probability be viewed as the pavement in the central courtyard of the Antonia.

67 Crucifixion. Fresco in the chapel of Sts. Cyricus and Julitta in the church of S. Maria Antiqua at Rome. Donated by Theodotus; executed before 741.

68 Tomb in Bethphage, not far from Bethany (on the eastern slope of Mt. Olivet near Jerusalem); example of a type of rock tomb, to be found in the Holy Land, which could be sealed off by rolling a large stone down the passageway. The most famous example of this kind of tomb, used by important Jews, is the tomb of "Herod's Family" which Flavius Josephus mentions and which is still well preserved in Jerusalem extra muros ["outside the walls"]. The discovery of such "roll tombs" made intelligible the references in Matthew (27:60) and Luke (24:1-2) concerning Jesus' tomb.

72 The unbelieving Thomas. Representation in niello on the outside of a chalice with handles in the monastery of Wilten. Diameter of the hemispheric-shaped cup, 5.85 inches; height of foot and knob, 3.32 inches.

69 Resurrection of Christ. Enamel panel (thirteenth in the middle row), part of the altar ornamentation done by Nicholas of Verdun (born in Verdun probably around 1130, certainly before 1150; died after 1205, probably at Tournai). The fifty-one panels are all of enamel, chiefly champlevé; the metal substratum is copper, the smooth surface of the unenameled parts is gilded. Date: 1181. Height of the whole set of pictures (exclusive of the wooden border) is 41.32 inches; length of central section, 102.6 inches; length of side panels, 47 inches each. The whole altar is the expression of a medieval theology of history in which Byzantine models are reinterpreted. Klosterneuburg (Augustinian Canons).

73 Ascension of Christ. Enamel panel (fourteenth in central row) by Nicholas of Verdun. Cf. note on picture no. 69.

70 The woman and the angel at the tomb. Relief in chased gold on the antependium (Pala d'Oro) before the high altar in the Cathedral of Aachen. Produced at Fulda around 1020 as a gift from Emperor Henry II. Frequently restored, most recently in 1951. Height of whole antependium, 50.3 inches; length 68.64 inches.

74 Pentecost. Limoges enamel (champlevé on gilded copper) from the gable of the reliquary of St. Anianus. The reliquary (thirteenth century) has the shape of a gabled house; when opened out it resembles a triptych, when closed, a tabernacle. On the outer panels the twelve apostles are shown receiving the Holy Spirit; from two hands held over them red flames (shown here) descend against a blue enamel background. The reliquary decorated with precious stones (on a wooden base), was originally a tabernacle (?), perhaps in the church of Saint Aignan in Chartres. Width, 26.9 inches (closed) and 30.8 inches (open); height, 30.8 inches; depth, 11.39 inches. In the Treasury of the Cathedral of Chartres.

71 Christ and the disciples at Emmaus. Enamel on gold, with tiny spiral embellishments. Front side (outside right) of a thirteenth-century reliquary. Length, 10.92 inches; height, 7.5 inches; depth, 4.9 inches. In the church at Nantouillet (Seine-et-Marne).

75 Christ enthroned. A figure of gilded copper, chased and incised; eyes of blue glass-flux; turquoise colored ornamentation of glass-flux. Made at Limoges in second quarter of thirteenth century. In the Schnütgenmuseum at Cologne, G 560.